DIY KOMBUCHA

HI, KOMBUCHA LOVER

It's true we just met, but there's an elephant in the room. Or more like a gelatinous blob. And we need to talk about it before deciding if we're going to make delicious kombucha together. It's the SCOBY.

- If the thought of a SCOBY makes your stomach turn a little, go to page **13** to understand where your future friend is coming from.

- If you're already down with your SCOBY, jump to page **36** to make your first master kombucha tea.

- If you and your SCOBY have made a lifelong commitment, start experimenting with healthy and flavorful infusions on page **51**.

Happy brewing!

KATHERINE GREEN

DIY KOMBUCHA

60 NOURISHING TONICS FOR HEALTH & HAPPINESS

in collaboration with

R
ROCKRIDGE PRESS

For general information on our other products and services or to obtain technical support, please contact our Customer Care Department within the United States at (866) 744-2665, or outside the United States at (510) 253-0500.

Rockridge Press publishes its books in a variety of electronic and print formats. Some content that appears in print may not be available in electronic books, and vice versa.

TRADEMARKS: Rockridge Press and the Rockridge Press logo are trademarks or registered trademarks of Callisto Media Inc. and/or its affiliates, in the United States and other countries, and may not be used without written permission. All other trademarks are the property of their respective owners. Rockridge Press is not associated with any product or vendor mentioned in this book.

Photography © 2015 by Shannon Oslick
Illustrations © 2015 by Tom Bingham

ISBN: Print 978-1-62315-475-2 | eBook 978-1-62315-476-9

CONTENTS

FOREWORD

Every kombucha brewer has an origin story. I refer to mine as the pear fiasco, but it could equally be called the pear miracle.

Five years ago I started my kombucha business in San Francisco. In the beginning, I sold my brew at farmers' markets and depended on those sales to keep brewing. My clientele gave me flack because I used white sugar in my kombucha, which I now know is absolutely irreplaceable. But I was a novice trying to get my business off the ground, so I went looking for a sugar alternative.

A local farmer told me to try using pears since their natural sugar content is quite high. He gave me four boxes of overly ripe pears and I got to boiling and pureeing them right away. I won't mince words: substituting pear sauce for sugar resulted in an undrinkable bucket of tea. However, I had an inspiration. I added the pear sauce to a finished batch of regular kombucha made with gunpowder green tea, a smoky tea that is perfectly balanced by the pears. I didn't find a way around using sugar, but I managed to create a new, delicious brew.

Smoked Pear sold out everywhere we introduced it. But there were two big problems. The sugar from the pears caused bottles to explode upon opening and the numerous boxes of ripe pears in our tiny space compounded pre-existing fruit fly issues. The stress of trying to meet demand, manage the fruit flies, and attend to customer complaints got to me. With both relief and regret, we put an end to Smoked Pear, the inspired and beloved brew that put the House Kombucha name on the map, but almost broke me in the process.

Your kombucha journey is about to begin. There will be successes and failures. Hopefully there will be a lot of experimentation, too. Follow the instructions and recipes laid out in these pages just enough to figure out how to deviate from them. For me, making kombucha has involved a whole lot of trial and error, and a whole lot of luck.

I am grateful to have been able to grow my business each year, but I can assure you of this: nothing tastes better than your homemade batch. Try as we may, no commercial producer can guarantee that each piece of fruit we use is perfectly ripened. As a do-it-yourself home brewer, you can ensure that only the best ingredients go into your kombucha.

From my family's kitchen to yours, may your homemade brews be filled with new experiences, rich tastes and smells, and may they serve as catalysts for your own unique stories.

Rana Chang
Owner/Founder, House Kombucha
www.housekombucha.com

AN EXPLORATION OF BUBBLY GOODNESS

I

1
KOMBUCHA FOR HEALTH AND HAPPINESS

Kombucha. 'Buch. Mushroom tea. Tea kvass. Whatever you call it, you know that it tastes great and offers numerous health benefits. What you may not know, however, is just how simple it is to take a DIY approach to this probiotic and immune-boosting powerhouse. If you're planning to use this book to get your feet wet, you've picked up an ideal step-by-step guide. If you've got a lot of experience making basic brews, this book is a good match for you too. Feel free to skip the introductory chapters and jump right in to the creative recipes for infusions, juices, smoothies, and even mocktails. Ideally, this is the one and only book you'll ever need to make kombucha for every season, every symptom, and every Sunday brunch.

FROM THE MASTERS

JARED ENGLUND
CO-FOUNDER OF LION HEART KOMBUCHA
www.lionheartkombucha.com

Allergies, indigestion, illness. More and more, imbalances plague our bodies, and yet we don't know why. For me, drinking kombucha was a big step in the direction of healing my gut, detoxifying my body, and being more in touch with where my food comes from.

My kombucha journey began with obsessive home brewing. After some time, I began to teach kombucha-making classes to others from my home. Today, I am a professional kombucha brewer. What I have come to learn is that, just like a healthy batch of kombucha, we need to see our bodies as "symbiotic colonies." We need to take care of the bacteria in our gut, realizing that bacteria aren't all bad. Our inner colonies need us to eat foods that encourage a healthy, balanced "ecosystem," and to stay active too. My path has led me to source food from local farmers, eat raw and probiotic foods daily, and regularly exercise in the form of biking and yoga practice.

I'm just one person, but I truly believe that we can make change to our bodies and our communities one day at a time, one person at a time, and even one kombucha at a time.

A TANGY TONIC FOR EVERY DAY

Today kombucha is commercially sold at many grocery stores and health food stores in a wide variety of flavors. It is most often infused with fruits, herbs, spices, and other flavorings to enhance its naturally sour taste. While its accessibility at your favorite store may make buying kombucha a no-brainer, you may be surprised to know just how easily and inexpensively it can be brewed at home, as it has been around the world for centuries.

As in all living things, kombucha begins with a "mother." A live starter culture, the "mother," or SCOBY, which stands for *symbiotic colony of bacteria and yeast.* The SCOBY is a gelatinous blob that bears a striking resemblance to a pancake. Because it also looks similar to a mushroom cap, kombucha is sometimes referred to as "mushroom tea." Thanks to the SCOBY, rather ordinary sweetened tea can be fermented into a probiotic masterpiece in about a week.

Fermentation is most recognized for its ability to create alcoholic beverages such as wine, beer, and mead. However, the process has also been used for centuries to preserve foods such as cucumbers and cabbage by converting them into their ever-tasty cousins: pickles and sauerkraut. Defined simply as the transformation of food items using various types of bacteria and fungi, fermentation can take many forms.

Factors such as fermentation length, the amount of sugar used, and the temperature during fermentation play a role in the finished kombucha's flavor spectrum that can land anywhere on a scale of sweet to puckeringly sour. What is always constant, though, is its makeup of living cultures, vitamins, and acids that can help support healthy digestion and increase energy.

Much like in yogurt making, the transformation process of fermentation leaves kombucha loaded with living organisms and active cultures that make it a solid nutritional source. Capable of balancing the good and bad bacteria that flourish in the intestinal tract, kombucha has been hailed as a magical tonic throughout its history. However, due to the conventions of research funding, it has never been studied at length on a scientific level in the United States, making its purported benefits largely anecdotal.

KOMBUCHA THEN AND NOW

Called "the tea of immortality" by the ancient Chinese, kombucha has a long past that is rife with whimsical stories of its origins and uses. It is brewed throughout Asia and Eastern Europe, and lore indicates that kombucha SCOBYs have been passed down within families and villages for countless generations.

Thought to have made its first appearance during the Chinese Qin dynasty of the third century BC, kombucha had its first boom as trade routes extended into India and Russia. The energizing tea is said to have improved the vitality of long-marching armies, travelers, and traders.

The elixir grew in popularity, and in AD 415, a Korean physician named Dr. Kombu reportedly brought it to Japan. Because *cha* is the

Japanese word for tea, stories suggest that kombucha was named after this doctor, who treated Japanese emperor Inyoko with the invigorating drink. Once widely used by samurai, the fermented tea is still popular in Japan to this day.

From Russia kombucha was introduced into Germany at the turn of the twentieth century, where it remained a popular beverage until World War II brought a shortage of tea and sugar.

In the United States kombucha had a small following in the 1960s and 1970s, when it was commonly called "hippie tea" and brewed at home. It has since surged in popularity, spawning a whole new generation of home brewers. In 2004, Whole Foods began the national distribution of a leading brand of kombucha, GT's Kombucha, and the craze really took off. The production of kombucha has led to a sizable cottage industry of kombucha manufacturers in hotspots like the San Francisco Bay Area; Portland, Oregon; and Brooklyn, New York.

At a time when the ill health effects of sugary sodas have hit the proverbial fan, a consistent rise in healthy, functional beverages such as kombucha, vitamin waters, and enhanced fruit drinks continues to gain traction. Kombucha's popularity has been spurred somewhat by the media craze for it, with high-profile celebrities being photographed drinking kombucha and medical experts on television touting it as a viable replacement for fructose-laden sodas.

Depending on where you live, you may be able to find kombucha locally on tap at stores and businesses in your neighborhood. From coast to coast, countless small manufacturers are making a business of selling kombucha, both bottled and in kegs.

Brewing kombucha is completely approachable and doable. Don't let the mystery surrounding this ancient beverage stop you from creating your own brews, chock-full of your favorite flavorings and accented with your own personal touch. An emerging community of talented professional and home brewers lead the way, proving that this old-world craft has an important place in these fast-paced times.

IT DOES A BODY GOOD

The benefits of kombucha are far-reaching and significant, according to regular drinkers. At the very least, it is an energizing and healthy beverage, low in sugar when compared with sodas and other beverages sweetened with high-fructose corn syrup. For this reason alone, and of course because it tastes great, it should be a regular part of a balanced diet.

Realistically, you should not set off on your kombucha-brewing journey with goals of curing disease and preventing aging. While the health benefits of the drink are many, it is, first and foremost, a refreshing beverage that can be enjoyed any number of ways. By adding herbs, spices, fruits, and vegetables to it, you can further increase its nutritional profile. It is, however, not a panacea for whatever ails you. Instead, it is a strong component of a healthy lifestyle and diet that can improve your overall wellness when used regularly.

Anecdotal evidence supports that kombucha can help:

* Detoxify the liver
* Prevent and treat arthritis

- Improve digestion
- Boost immunity
- Increase energy
- Improve metabolism
- Decrease symptoms of PMS
- Improve complexion
- Cure hangovers and headaches
- Support diabetes management

While scientific "proof" of these abilities is scarce to nonexistent, regular drinkers of kombucha swear by its abilities to help manage these conditions. Looking at what's inside kombucha is perhaps the best way to explain how this simple and tasty beverage can potentially do so many things within the body.

THE GOOD STUFF IN KOMBUCHA

Kombucha is packed with a healthy dose of vitamin C and several B vitamins, as well as many other powerful immune-boosting compounds. Probiotics make up a large aspect of kombucha's immunity-boosting abilities, and kombucha's ability to detoxify the liver is said to boost immunity and increase metabolism and energy. Additionally, the B vitamins play a minor role in immune function. Let's start with the vitamins, because these are so important to your health and vitality.

VITAMINS According to a 2000 study published in the *International Journal of Food Science and Technology*, kombucha has significant levels of B_1, B_6, and B_{12} vitamins, as well as the ever-important vitamin C. When you take a look at what these vitamins are responsible for in the

FAQ: HOW MUCH KOMBUCHA SHOULD I DRINK A DAY?

It depends. When you first start drinking kombucha, begin with just 4 ounces (½ cup) per day. Once you have adjusted to drinking kombucha regularly, it can be incorporated into your diet in 4- to 8-ounce increments two times per day.

Space out your consumption of kombucha to ensure that your body has adequate time to absorb its available vitamins and amino acids, and drink plenty of water in addition to kombucha to flush toxins from your body.

Keep in mind that in the case of kombucha, more is not better. According to the American Nutrition Association, daily intake of kombucha should be capped at 16 ounces.

body, it begins to make sense that the nutrient boost from regularly drinking kombucha can provide such health-enhancing results.

Most notable for their ability to turn food into energy, B vitamins are a necessary component of any diet to maintain a healthy liver, skin, hair, and eyes. B_1, commonly called the "anti-stress vitamin," is thought to strengthen the body's immune system by improving its response to stress, according to the University of Maryland Medical Center. B_6 helps your body use protein, supports brain function, and helps build red blood cells. Meanwhile, vitamin B_{12} plays an integral role in cell metabolism, nerve function, and red blood cell formation, according to the Mayo Clinic.

Vitamin C, a powerful antioxidant itself, has been shown in studies to lower rates of cancer and heart disease when included in the diet, according to the Mayo Clinic. Sounds good, right? Well, there's more—much more.

PROBIOTICS Beyond the vitamins, there are the yeasts and bacteria that make kombucha so beneficial for the body. According to the Cultures for Health website, kombucha always contains acetobacter, Saccharomyces, and Brettanomyces, as well as amino acids and esters and many other variable strains of yeast and bacteria.

According to WebMD, these living organisms, called probiotics, are beneficial in keeping the intestines healthy and aiding in digestion. Probiotics have been studied extensively, and current evidence points toward their ability to improve overall intestinal function, maintain a strong immune system, and treat a number of ailments, including diarrhea, ulcerative colitis, and even eczema.

FAQ: HOW MUCH ALCOHOL IS IN KOMBUCHA?

Kombucha is not a 100 percent alcohol-free beverage, but unless you intentionally take steps to up its alcoholic content, you'll never get close to feeling a buzz. The typical alcohol level in finished kombucha hovers around 0.5 percent ABV (alcohol by volume) after it ferments for about a week. This is similar to the amount found in nonalcoholic beer.

Alcohol levels stay low because the kombucha ferments during the first several days in a vessel that's not airtight. When oxygen is in contact with the kombucha, it works to convert alcohol into acetobacter, commonly called acetic acid, which is the compound responsible for the vinegary taste of kombucha.

Some kombucha brewers want more than just a basic tea. They're looking for a fizzy beverage that resembles soda. The same process that adds fizz to the beverage—called secondary fermentation, discussed in detail in chapter 2—increases the alcoholic content. Once the container is sealed, such as after bottling, acetobacter has no access to oxygen, and the sugars more readily convert into alcohol. If secondary fermentation is extended for long periods (that is, for several weeks) and a sugary substance such as fruit juice is used to start the fermentation, a kombucha's ABV can increase to as high as 3 percent.

To keep the alcohol content low, limit secondary fermentation to 48 hours, then promptly refrigerate the kombucha to halt the fermentation process. Also, stick with flavorings that do not have large amounts of sugar, as these can contribute to higher alcohol levels because bacteria and yeast feed on sugar to create alcohol. Instead, use herbs, spices, and other ingredients that do not contain additional sugars, to add flavor to your kombucha.

BE YOUR OWN BREWMASTER

Everyone's journey to home brewing kombucha is different. Whether you are simply interested in replicating your favorite commercial blend, desire to be more self-sustainable, or are working to decrease the sugar in your diet, there are countless motivations to get involved with the home-brewing process. Here are the top five reasons to become a kombucha DIYer.

1. **It's empowering.** Just like nurturing and growing a sourdough culture is an act of science, so is your kombucha home brew. Learning the craft of fermentation is something you can do to advance your knowledge of the craft and make you all the more self-sustainable. Take control of your health and well-being by making an endless supply of kombucha in your own kitchen, no matter the size of the space or time of year.

2. **It saves you money.** If you have a habit of buying kombucha at the grocery store, health food store, or from the tap, you undoubtedly have realized that the cost adds up fast. Not so when you make it at home. Requiring just sugar, water, tea, and the initial cost of a SCOBY (or get one from a friend!), you can save significant money making kombucha on your own.

3. **It gives you control.** Once you have the basics down, you can easily tweak the master recipe by adding your favorite flavors to create a kombucha that is suited to your own palate. Whether you prefer the strong kick of ginger or jalapeño, or a smooth fruit flavor, it's in your hands when you home brew kombucha.

4. **It's simple.** This book has a large swath of recipes to create some really tasty drinks, but that is just so that you have plenty of options for enjoying your newly made kombucha. Don't think this is too complicated or get overwhelmed by the process. Kombucha should not be shrouded in difficulty or complication.

5. **It's ridiculously fun.** Kombucha brewing is an entertaining activity to get your creative juices flowing and nourish the science geek hiding inside you. Once you begin this simple fermentation, you may find you really enjoy the passive work of keeping your tea going and delve into one or many of the other fermenting arts for improved health.

DRINKS, DRINKS, AND MORE DRINKS

Once you have the basics under your belt, don't stop there. There is so much more to learn. Starting with the master recipe, come on a journey of drink mixing that ranges from sweet and refreshing to filling and savory. Combining nutrient-boosting ingredients such as herbs, spices, fruits, and vegetables, these drinks are formulated to build on the inherent health benefits of kombucha itself.

The recipes are organized by type of kombucha drink, and there is something for everyone here. Start your day with a nutritious kombucha smoothie, or enjoy fruity, effervescent kombucha in the afternoon for a quick pick-me-up. When nighttime comes, whip up a mocktail for a healthy alternative to alcohol.

Explore the tips included with each recipe for more information on the health benefits of the ingredients, possible substitutions, and other related information that can help on your journey to improved health. Use these recipes for a new way to get valuable vitamins and nutrients into your diet and make the most of your kombucha brew.

FAQ: IS BREWING KOMBUCHA DANGEROUS?

There has been some media attention over the years about the dangers of brewing kombucha at home. However, when brewed properly, there are very few risks to making kombucha on your own. After all, people have been making it for hundreds of years, and modern-day sanitation is much greater than it was way back when.

Cleanliness is paramount, and knowing how to recognize any problems can go a long way toward protecting your brew and your health. As a general rule, if something looks or smells off, it probably is. Trust your instincts. In chapter 3, troubleshooting your brew is covered. Read this before you get started to dispel any fears. Arm yourself with the knowledge to recognize problems and act appropriately.

People all over the world brew kombucha at home without any danger to their health. As long as you practice good hand washing, avoid cross contamination in the kitchen, and monitor your brew regularly, you can all but guarantee your success.

FROM THE MASTERS

DAINA SLEKYS TROUT, MS MPH
CEO & FOUNDER OF HEALTH-ADE LLC
www.health-ade.com

Kombucha is enjoyed by countless cultures across the globe and existed long before any of the stereotypes that now prevail existed. I have friends in music, fashion, science, art, medicine, sales, finance, and politics that swear by it.

When you embark on brewing your own, keep this in mind:

1. Most of us don't get it right the first time! Keep at it. I am always tweaking my recipe, even a decade later.

2. Play around with the amounts and ingredients until you get what you like. There are many ways to make your kombucha delicious.

3. Only use the best-quality SCOBY that you can get your hands on. For home brews, I recommend those from KombuchaKamp.com.

4. High-quality, organic ingredients are a must. Don't mess around with anything that's processed. It may sound weird and wacky, but I swear that the kombucha holds a grudge if you expose it to anything unnatural.

2

YOUR KOMBUCHA KITCHEN

To get started making kombucha, all you need to do is stock your kitchen with a few essential pieces of equipment and a handful of ingredients. As with any venture, you can start small and scale up your operation as your confidence and know-how grow. Following are the must-haves that will ensure your success as you begin this age-old fermentation project.

CORE INGREDIENTS

All the kombucha drinks in this book begin with the Master Kombucha Tea recipe (see page 36). This recipe uses one of three distinct teas—green, black, or oolong—to create a base, free of any flavorings, infusions, or soda-like effervescence. To make a master kombucha tea, you need just five standard ingredients: tea, sugar, starter tea, SCOBY, and water. Every batch you make starts with these, and getting these elements right from the start will help you create a successful brew that tastes great every time.

TEA

Tea is the cornerstone of your kombucha brewing process, and your choices are pretty wide open. Choose from the many varieties of black, green, oolong, and white teas widely available from a number of manufacturers. Or better yet, use a combination of teas to create a unique blend. Either way, the key is to choose a tea made from the plant *Camellia sinensis*, and not an herbal blend, as this is a key element to the fermentation process. One important factor to note is that the amount of caffeine in your tea will remain constant throughout the brewing process. Black teas are the highest in caffeine (60 to 90 mg), while white and green teas (30 to 70 mg) are the lowest, and oolong tea falls right in the middle (50 to 75 mg).

The master kombucha recipe at the end of the chapter provides information for brewing with black, green, and oolong teas, but white teas can be used for brewing as well. They make a fruity, sweet kombucha that appeals to those

who dislike the strong taste of other kombucha varieties. White teas are usually very expensive, as they are made from young buds picked from the tea plant. Once picked, they then are allowed to wither in the sun before processing. The best steeping temperature for white teas is 160°F to 180°F.

BLACK TEA creates a kombucha with strong woody tones and a higher caffeine count than green or oolong teas. Popular black teas used for kombucha include Darjeeling, orange pekoe, and English breakfast blends. While the taste of each is distinct on its own, the one thing they all have in common is that their long-term consumption can help prevent stroke, reduce the risk of several types of cancer, and boost the immune system. Try one type of black tea alone, or blend two or more favorites for a unique brew that stands out as all your own.

GREEN TEA creates a lighter, slightly sweeter kombucha that's great for blended drinks and infusions. Green teas also finish fermenting a bit quicker than other types of tea, so don't let this prized blend go unattended for too long.

OOLONG, the Cadillac of teas, makes a stunningly complex kombucha that boasts additional nutrients and acids not found in black and green teas. The flavors of a finished oolong tea kombucha can vary widely, from having woody tones to bright, almost sweetened honey-like notes. While oolong tea is by far the most expensive of the three teas used here, it creates a truly distinct kombucha.

SUGAR

Pure cane sugar is the sweetener of choice in most kombucha making. This is such an important element, as the sugar is what feeds the SCOBY and helps it ferment the tea. While concerns about sugar intake may fuel your desire to cut back on it or find an alternative, know that this sugar is not for you—it's for the hungry microbes. Only about 1 percent of the starting amount of sugar remains in the finished brew. Avoid the use of artificial sweeteners, as these are never recommended for brewing kombucha.

STARTER TEA

Starter tea is essential to lowering the pH of your sweetened tea to protect it from microbial invasion, as well as to add helpful yeasts and bacteria to the brew to boost fermentation. Once you get your brew going, you will save at least 2 cups of the tea each time with your SCOBY so that you always have this starter tea ready to jumpstart your next batch. Starter tea can be store-bought raw kombucha that is free of any flavoring or infusion.

SCOBY

Then there is the prize of the whole process— your SCOBY. Due to kombucha's growing popularity, SCOBYs are increasingly easier to come across. SCOBYs can be sourced through a number of online retailers in both dehydrated and fresh forms. See the Resources section for

suppliers. Reconstitute dehydrated SCOBY before brewing, following the directions that come with the SCOBY to do so. Alternatively, get a SCOBY from a friend or from any number of online or local kombucha-brewing communities that give them away for free or trade.

Whatever your source, be sure it comes from a well-maintained, clean place. When you get your SCOBY, keep it healthy by sealing it in a container filled with kombucha (your starter tea) until you are ready to brew. Keep it in the refrigerator to slow down its metabolic rate until you are ready to begin your brew. Just bring it to room temperature before adding it to the sweetened tea.

WATER

While it is not immediately noticeable in each brew, water quality plays a significant role in the health and taste of your kombucha. Most city water systems add chlorine and fluoride to the water supply, both of which can cause the environment of your SCOBY to suffer. Filtered or bottled water are the best options. However, leaving a pot of tap water on the counter for 24 hours allows the chlorine to evaporate, and this is typically sufficient for creating and maintaining a great brew. Fluoride does not evaporate, and there is some school of thought that it can negatively affect your SCOBY over time.

ESSENTIAL EQUIPMENT

There are some specific pieces of equipment that are necessary for getting started on your home brew. Rather simple and inexpensive, the supplies should take up little space in your kitchen and should not be difficult to source if you don't have them already. Once you've gathered these items, you're ready to get started putting your SCOBY to work for you.

BREWING EQUIPMENT

There are three pieces of brewing equipment you'll need: a fermentation vessel, a thermometer, and a cotton cloth.

FERMENTATION VESSEL The most important of the equipment is a suitable brewing jar, ideally made of glass. Metal can leach unsafe elements that can harm a SCOBY and your health and should therefore be avoided. Food-grade plastic is an option, as is nonleaded ceramic. Glass, however, is the vessel of choice, and it should be easy to find. An ideal jar will have a wide mouth, leaving plenty of room for oxygen exchange with the surface of the tea. The more room your SCOBY has to grow, the faster the fermentation process will be. Aim for a jar that is wide enough at the very least to stick your entire hand in, as you will need to put your SCOBY into and take it out of the jar. Look for a suitable jar at any store where canning supplies are sold. There are many types of gallon-size glass jars on the market that will work. If you cannot find one, two half-gallon canning jars will work as well.

THERMOMETER This is a vital tool for ensuring that your sweetened tea is at the right temperature to begin fermentation. Skipping this step can result in the death of your SCOBY and starter tea and can even introduce the dreaded invader—mold. An instant-read thermometer is the tool of choice; however, a

PRIMARY FERMENTATION PRIMER

Primary fermentation is the process that creates kombucha. Bacteria and yeasts feed on sugar, and once you introduce them to their new home in a batch of sweet tea, they quickly go to work. Due to its high sugar content, sweetened tea is the ideal environment for their survival. Unlike other ferments such as sourdough or pickles that rely on wild yeast and bacteria to transform them, kombucha is purposefully inoculated with a starter culture in the same way that wine and beer are inoculated with yeast.

Once these bacteria and yeasts are introduced by way of the SCOBY, they get to work transforming the sweetened tea into a blend of enzymes and acids. The longer the process is allowed to go, the further they will transform the tea from sweet to markedly sour. Somewhere in between, when your palate finds the taste pleasing, you end primary fermentation by removing the SCOBY and refrigerating the kombucha to stop the metabolic processes of the still-present bacteria and yeast.

sticky thermometer that attaches to the outside of your fermentation vessel is also a good indicator.

COTTON CLOTH Kombucha needs to breathe, and all bugs, including ants and fruit flies, need to stay out. Enter the cotton cloth barrier. Avoid using cheesecloth, as its porous holes make it subject to pesky invasions. Choose instead a cotton cloth with a very fine weave. A clean dishtowel, cotton T-shirt, or pillowcase are all functional covers that keep the bad stuff out while still allowing an easy interchange of oxygen so the SCOBY can feed and grow. You will need a rubber band to secure the cloth onto the rim of the fermentation vessel.

BOTTLING EQUIPMENT

You'll be using bottles to house your finished brews. All bottles are not the same, and care must be taken to select bottles suitable for handling the pressure that will build in them—especially if you plan on performing secondary fermentation. Any bottle with a screw cap that originally held a carbonated beverage is suitable for use. Or, you can purchase new pressure-capable bottles from a home-brew shop in your area. Flip-top glass bottles, such as those that Grolsch beer is bottled in, are a favorite among kombucha brewers. They can withstand pressure, are reusable, and do not require capping. Alternatively, some people use plastic, especially for secondary fermentation, so that they are able to feel the pressure buildup on the bottle, giving them a good indication of when it is time to place the bottles in the refrigerator and end fermentation.

FAQ: WHERE CAN I BUY BOTTLING EQUIPMENT?

A home-brew shop is your best option for purchasing the equipment you need for bottling kombucha. Whether you have one in your town or not, many are now online and have a complete inventory of all the supplies you would ever need. Check out the Resources section for some retailers with a good inventory of bottling supplies. Reusing flip-top beer bottles and growlers is another option that makes the process all the more economical. Also, many bottling supplies can be sourced from websites like Craigslist, where you can purchase or trade bottling supplies with others for a good cost. Whether buying new or used bottling equipment, always make sure to clean it thoroughly before using.

ODDS AND ENDS

You will also need to gather a few more supplies, most of which you likely have readily available in your kitchen. To start, you will need a 6- or 8-quart stainless steel pot and lid for brewing the tea. You will also need a slotted spoon, funnel, fine-mesh strainer, and a set of measuring cups. Before you begin, wash all equipment that will come in contact with the kombucha with warm, soapy water, rinsing well to remove any soap residue. Avoid the use of antibacterial agents when cleaning your equipment, as these can inhibit or even kill your SCOBY and its valuable microbes. Be sure to rinse all equipment thoroughly after washing and allow it to air-dry.

INFUSION INGREDIENTS

Once you have created your brew, the possibilities for flavoring it are endless. Anything from juices, fruits, and vegetables to spices and herbs is fair game when it comes to adding flavor and style to your brew. From simple, one-flavor additions to complex, multi-ingredient infusions, the possibilities are as vast as your own imagination. Additionally, you can add secondary fermentation to the mix and create kombucha blends with all the effervescence of a soda while still maintaining the health benefits of kombucha. And the bonus is: They contain way less sugar than soda and still taste amazing.

By adding fresh, seasonal fruits and vegetables to your kombucha juice or smoothie blends, you can increase their health benefits. In some cases, these additions can even satisfy one or more of your five recommended daily servings of fresh fruits and vegetables. Whether you infuse fruits, vegetables, herbs, and spices into your kombucha or simply add them to a smoothie, try various flavor combinations to really unlock some of the amazing ways kombucha can be dressed up. All of the recipes in this book use flavorings that are added after the primary fermentation stage.

YOUR FLAVORING PANTRY

The kombucha brewer's flavoring pantry need not be extensive, but here's a short list of fruits, vegetables, herbs, and spices that are especially versatile and worth having on hand.

FRUITS Fruits are a great way to add sweetness to your raw kombucha while providing a good amount of sugar to jumpstart secondary fermentation. Fruits can be added in their raw, whole state; puréed; juiced; or as an extract

SECONDARY FERMENTATION PRIMER

Secondary fermentation is the process of refermenting the kombucha once it's bottled. The process has two results. The first is that it produces carbonation. Carbon dioxide, a by-product of fermentation, cannot escape once the kombucha is sealed in an airtight environment. It therefore disperses among the kombucha to create a bubbly beverage much like soda.

The second purpose of secondary fermentation is to flavor the kombucha with additional elements not included during primary fermentation.

Flavorings are added at this stage after the SCOBY has been removed. It's crucial to remove the SCOBY to prevent damage to it and the creation of off-flavors in it from these additional ingredients. While it is possible in some cases to flavor kombucha during the primary fermentation stage, this adversely affects the SCOBY and is not typically recommended unless you plan on discarding the SCOBY after use.

flavoring. Some popular fruits to pair with kombucha include:

- Açai berries
- Blackberries
- Blueberries
- Grapes
- Grapefruit
- Lemons
- Limes
- Oranges
- Peaches

Whole fruits, purées, and extracts are the best choice for secondary fermentation, especially when using fruits with a high sugar content. Keep in mind that adding juices such as apple and grape juice can increase the alcohol level in kombucha during secondary fermentation due to concentrated levels of sugar in the juice.

VEGETABLES Vegetables can lend a distinct flavor to kombucha and create a stunning drink in their own right. Commonly added in either juice or purée form, vegetables don't have high levels of added sugar and are a good choice for secondary fermentation when you're trying to keep alcohol content low. Some typical vegetables added to kombucha for secondary fermentation include:

- Beets
- Carrots
- Cucumbers
- Tomatoes

If you're not planning a secondary fermentation of your kombucha, consider adding one of the following:

- Avocado
- Kale
- Spinach
- Tomatillos

These make great additions to smoothies, in particular, and pack a nutritional punch.

HERBS Delicate and light, fresh or dried herbs can add a memorable infusion of flavor to your kombucha, in addition to their natural healing properties. They can be added as part of a blend or simply on their own during secondary fermentation to create a drink that pops with flavor. Alternatively, you can simply steep refrigerated kombucha with herbs in it to create a flavorful blend without the added work of secondary fermentation. Recommended herbs for kombucha flavoring include:

- Basil
- Chamomile
- Elderflowers
- Lemon balm
- Mint
- Rosemary
- Sage

SPICES Whole, dried, or fresh spices are the final must-have in your kombucha pantry. Like herbs, these can either be added as part of secondary fermentation or steeped in the finished kombucha while refrigerated to lend additional flavor. A little goes a long way with most spices, so don't go crazy with these kombucha additions.

- Cardamom
- Cinnamon
- Cloves
- Fennel seeds
- Ginger, fresh (the most commonly used)
- Vanilla beans

You can also use roots such as birch, burdock, sarsaparilla, and sassafras to create a naturally flavored root beer, as well as many other drinks.

3

YOUR FIRST BREW

You've gathered all the equipment and supplies, but now what? Take a deep breath and get ready to kick off your first batch of kombucha. This simple craft is about to be unraveled in a matter of a few pages, and you will be ready to begin on your own, treading forward toward a master brew with complexity and punch. Follow along and get brewing!

PREPARING TO BREW

Before you get started, keep in mind:

- **Practice makes perfect.** It typically takes a couple of cycles until you reach your natural rhythm and figure out how to make kombucha just how you like it. Your first brew will not be your best. Don't get discouraged if your first batch is not perfect. Keep at it until you like the results.

- **Make sure all the equipment that will come in contact with your SCOBY and starter tea is cleaned well.** While it is not necessary to sanitize all the equipment like in wine or beer making, it is important that it does not have any food particles or other residues on it that can negatively affect the SCOBY. Wash all utensils and equipment in warm, soapy water; rinse them well; and let them air-dry before beginning. Be sure there is no soapy residue left on any equipment, as this can interfere with the SCOBY.

- **Don't be concerned about the time this whole process will take.** While fermentation does take about a week in most cases, most of this is inactive time, meaning that there is little actual work to do to maintain the health of your SCOBY. Apart from the initial tea making, there is pretty much no other work involved. Set your kombucha to the side and don't spend too much time worrying about it. When fermentation time is up, check it out, and enjoy the fruits of your labor (or lack of labor)!

Let's go over what you need to have at your fingertips. It is helpful to arrange all the items you'll be using before beginning to streamline and simplify the process.

Your best bet is to start with a master recipe that uses black tea. This simple, versatile recipe will all but guarantee your success and the health of your new SCOBY. Once you have mastered black tea kombucha, you can play around with the green or oolong teas, or make your own using a blend of your favorite teas. You'll find the Master Kombucha Tea recipe at the end of this chapter.

EQUIPMENT

- Bottles
- Clean towel (for cleaning spills)
- Fermentation vessel
- Funnel
- Instant-read thermometer
- Measuring cup, dry
- Measuring cup, liquid
- Pot
- Rubber band
- Spoon
- Stove
- Tasting utensil
- White cloth cover

SUPPLIES

- SCOBY
- Starter tea
- Sugar
- Tea
- Water

EVALUATING AND BOTTLING YOUR BREW

Evaluating and bottling your kombucha are steps just as important as, if not more important than, making the brew itself. In fact, it's in these steps that the process can go off the rails. The key is cleanliness and avoiding cross-contamination at all costs. Skipping any step in these processes will likely result in spoiled kombucha that will have to be thrown out.

EVALUATING

Once your kombucha is fermenting, there are several indications that it is nearing completion. The first is your SCOBY. As the brew ferments, a new SCOBY will begin to form on its surface. Initially looking like small white spots, they will eventually form together and become both thicker and wider. If left to ferment for a long period, the white spots will eventually form into an entirely new patty.

When a new SCOBY develops, or after three to six days, it is time to taste your brew and determine whether it is ready for drinking. The strength of your starting culture and temperature in the fermenting location can affect the time it takes to get to this point. Tasting the developing kombucha around this time is recommended to get a feel for the fermentation process and how you prefer the kombucha to taste. Whether you prefer it on the sweeter end like in this early stage or when it is more tart after a few more days of fermentation is strictly personal preference. Two weeks is typically the maximum recommended brew time, and at this point, the kombucha can cross the line

from delicious to vinegar tasting within a matter of days.

Get a taste of your brew in one of three ways:

1. Place a straw into the kombucha, avoiding the SCOBY, and cap it with your finger to pull out a small amount of the kombucha to taste.

2. Press a small shot glass into the kombucha, depressing the SCOBY, to take a small amount of kombucha from the surface.

3. Use a wine thief (find this at a home-brewing store) to extract a sample of the kombucha. This device is specifically designed to sample a home brew or wine in a sanitary way without contaminating the batch.

Whichever method you use to sample the kombucha, make sure you use an implement that is clean and rinsed of any soap residue that could contaminate the batch.

BOTTLING

Your own personal tastes will dictate when to bottle your brew. As you evolve as a kombucha brewer, you will learn what you like and how to consistently achieve that preference. Typically, seven to nine days is the standard time it takes for kombucha to ferment into a delicious mixture of sweet and sour. However, if you plan on adding a sweet flavoring during fermentation, you may prefer to ferment the batch longer so that there is less available sugar at bottling. Conversely, if you plan on using secondary

SCOBY BETWEEN BREWS

Your SCOBY must be stored properly between brews. If you're planning to brew again within a week, the SCOBY and starter tea can be stored together in the refrigerator. Before using again, bring them to room temperature. If your next brew is more than a week away, the easiest way to store your SCOBY is to place it in a jar of sweetened tea at room temperature, about 72°F. Fill a quart-size glass jar with about 3½ cups room-temperature sweetened tea (3½ cups water, ¼ cup sugar, and 3 bags of tea), a bit of finished kombucha (¼ cup), and the SCOBY.

Cover the jar and place it in a location that is neither too hot nor too cold, as either can promote the growth of mold. If your SCOBY's naptime carries on for over a month, swap out some of the now-kombucha for more sweetened tea. This needs to be done roughly every month until you are ready to begin again. When you start fresh, separate the new baby SCOBY that has grown on your original SCOBY and save it as a backup in this same manner. Get two batches going at once, compost it, or give it away to a fellow brewer.

fermentation to add carbonation with no additional sweeteners, it is recommended that you bottle the batch when it is still noticeably sweet. While many factors come into play in creating your kombucha, your taste buds are the best judge of the right time for bottling.

When you have determined it's time for bottling, remove the SCOBY using clean hands and place it on a plate or in a jar covered with kombucha. Reserve two cups of kombucha (starter tea) as well for your next batch.

Prepare your bottles by cleaning them with warm, soapy water and rinsing them thoroughly. Allow them to air-dry. If you're adding flavorings for secondary fermentation, add these to the bottles before filling them with the kombucha. Place a funnel over the bottle and pour the kombucha into it, leaving about an inch of headspace

in the neck of the bottle. Tightly cap the bottles and refrigerate the kombucha to enjoy now, or leave them on the counter for another day or two to complete secondary fermentation.

There are many variables in the process of kombucha making that can leave you with a slightly different amount of tea once fully fermented. How much kombucha the added herbs, spices, and fruits absorb during infusion; natural evaporation; and differences in fill levels can play a role in these small variances. For this reason, recipes in this book do not have an exact number of bottles needed for each recipe. However, *when brewing kombucha by the gallon, you will typically need eight 16-ounce bottles.*

FROM THE MASTERS

RANA CHANG
OWNER/FOUNDER OF HOUSE KOMBUCHA
www.housekombucha.com

SCOBY growing out of control? Try brewing without one. You don't need the SCOBY to turn sweet tea into kombucha. What you do need is a good lively kombucha starter.

Kombucha starter can be made from a regular bottle of live kombucha. Just take a plain (no added juice, extracts, or sweeteners!) bottle of live raw kombucha, add ¼ cup of sugar, stir well, and leave it out at room temperature, covered with a secure piece of cloth for 1–2 weeks (depending on how warm your room is and the type of kombucha used). The sugar will ferment and the kombucha will become extra sour. A little SCOBY might even grow on top! Skim off the SCOBY and just use the sour kombucha as your starter.

If you already have a homebrew going, let a few cups of your kombucha hang out in the fermenter for a few extra days to get a super sour kombucha. Use this starter as you would in a regular kombucha recipe.

Remember, the starter needs to be more sour than a kombucha that you would drink. Adding the starter to the sweet tea needs to bring the new ferment to below pH 4 in order to keep the ferment safe from pathogenic growth.

If your kombucha starter is strong and alive, you will find that fermentation proceeds just fine without the SCOBY. Who would have thought?

TROUBLESHOOTING GUIDE

Your eyes and nose are the best indicators that something has run amok when brewing kombucha. Here are some of the most common problems you might face:

VINEGAR OVERLOAD

If your kombucha is left to ferment for too long, or under conditions that are too hot, you may taste it and nearly gag from a vinegar overload. This is most common in summer months, when ambient room temperatures soar just enough to really speed up fermentation. If this happens to you, don't worry—all is not lost. At least you have a robust SCOBY that is ready to get back to work. Start again and check your brew a bit earlier this time. Keep notes on the process, as well as air temperature, to determine whether a shorter fermentation time works better in your particular environment. And by all means, don't throw away the batch. Instead, use it in the same way as vinegar to flavor foods.

FRUIT FLIES

Fruit flies love kombucha, and your brew will naturally attract them, especially in the summer months when they can become a nuisance of great magnitude. Always keep your kombucha covered with a clean towel when not actively working with it, to prevent the flies from making a home in it. Just one trapped fruit fly can produce a whole family of fruit flies that will happily munch on your kombucha until they are fat and ready to start families of their own. If your kombucha becomes infested, toss the whole batch and start again. To prevent infestation, make an inexpensive DIY fruit fly trap by placing a small paper funnel in a cup with a bit of kombucha in it. They will fly in and be unable to escape. Place this next to your kombucha to prevent them from clinging to your brew's surface for dear life.

MOLD

Mold is the most common contaminator. Just like when it grows on cheese or bread, mold in kombucha takes on many colors and often appears to be fuzzy. Commonly, beginning brewers mistake new SCOBY formation as mold. However, unlike new SCOBY, mold always forms on the surface and will either be dry on the surface or look like something entirely different than the SCOBY. If you do think mold is to blame, check your specimen against countless pictures online to confirm what you are seeing. If you do determine that you have mold, toss the entire batch and start again. Mold typically grows when fermentation temperatures are too low, you under-acidified the batch at the beginning of fermentation, or you added the culture and SCOBY when the temperature was too hot, thereby killing it. Be sure to follow kombucha-brewing instructions and check the temperature of the sweetened tea before the start of fermentation to avoid growing mold.

OFF-FLAVORS

It's important to keep your kombucha away from other fermenting items in your kitchen, such as sauerkraut, pickles, and kimchi. Because these items all utilize natural yeasts and bacteria in the environment, it is possible that these differing strains of bacteria and yeast can get into and grow in your kombucha when stored in close proximity with one another. To prevent this and the associated off-flavors it can produce, store all other ferments away from kombucha in your kitchen.

Be sure to keep good notes on your process and any observations you encounter while making each batch of kombucha. This will ensure that you learn from mistakes, recognize patterns in your results, and in the end, are able to create a great brew consistently—each and every time you make kombucha.

MASTER KOMBUCHA TEA

MAKES 1 GALLON

This master recipe—with temperature and preparation specifics for black, green, or oolong tea—forms the base of all kombucha recipes. Don't be discouraged if your first few batches are not on par with commercial blends. It takes practice to learn to brew just how you like it, and master the amount of time it takes in your particular environment to create that flavor consistently. Experiment with the different types of teas to determine which you prefer, and keep good records of your process and the variables that can affect the end product.

A CLOSER LOOK

At some point in the fermentation process, you'll notice long chains forming on your SCOBY or freely floating around in your brew. These are yeast colonies. Don't worry—this is completely natural. To minimize their growth in future batches, strain them from the starter culture before using and rinse your SCOBY in clean water before use.

14 cups water, divided into 4 cups and 10 cups, at room temperature

8 standard-size tea bags or 17 grams loose tea (black, green, or oolong) in a diffuser

1 cup pure cane sugar

2 cups starter tea

1 SCOBY

DAY 1

1. In a small pot, heat 4 cups of water until just shy of a boil. Promptly turn off the heat.

For black tea, heat to between 200°F and 212°F.
For green tea, heat to between 170°F and 180°F.
For oolong tea, heat to between 190°F and 205°F.

2. Add the tea bags to the water and stir. Cover the pot and steep the tea for 5 minutes. Remove the lid and, using a spoon, press each tea bag against the side of the pot to extract as many nutrients as possible. Allow the tea bags to steep for another 5 minutes in the covered pot, then remove.

3. Add the sugar to the tea and stir until the sugar completely dissolves.

4. Transfer the sweetened tea to a clean 1-gallon fermentation vessel. Add the remaining 10 cups of water to the tea.

5. Using an instant-read thermometer, check the temperature of the tea. If it is below 85°F, proceed to step 6. If the temperature is 85°F or higher, cover the vessel with a clean white cloth and wait until the temperature drops.

6. Add the starter tea to the fermentation vessel. With clean, rinsed hands, gently place the SCOBY on top of the mixture. It does not matter if it floats, sinks, or hovers in the sweetened tea.

7. Cover the fermentation vessel with a clean white cloth, secure the top with a rubber band, and place the fermentation vessel in a location that is out of direct sunlight and can maintain a temperature above 68°F, preferably between 72°F and 82°F.

DAYS 3 TO 6

After 3 to 6 days, the SCOBY will have spread across the entire top of the liquid. When this occurs, it's time to take a taste. If the brew is too sweet, continue fermenting for a couple more days until you get the taste you desire. If it's just right, you're ready to proceed.

1. With clean hands, remove the SCOBY from the fermentation vessel, place it on a plate or in a bowl, and cover it with a bit of kombucha. Reserve 2 cups of kombucha starter tea for your next batch. Begin a new brew immediately or put your SCOBY to rest (see page 32) and refrigerate your reserved starter tea for up to 10 days.

2. Using a cleaned, thoroughly rinsed plastic funnel and spouted measuring cup, fill your bottles with kombucha, leaving about 1 inch of headspace in each bottle neck. Use a fine mesh strainer as you pour the kombucha to catch and dispose of any accumulated yeast strands. Close each bottle and cap tightly. At this point, you can either refrigerate the kombucha to end the fermentation process or proceed with secondary fermentation.

OPTIONAL SECONDARY FERMENTATION

1. Leave the bottles in a warm, dark location. The ideal temperature range is between 72°F and 78°F. While higher temperatures can also work, they will accelerate the fermentation process.

2. After 48 hours, refrigerate 1 bottle for at least 6 hours to thoroughly chill it. Never attempt to open a warm bottle, as it will be too bubbly and can explode.

3. Once chilled, pop the bottle open (over the sink) and pour your kombucha into a glass. If it is still too sweet or not bubbly enough, leave the unopened bottles for another day or two before trying again.

4. Once your desired flavor and effervescence are achieved, refrigerate the unopened bottles of kombucha. Continuing their fermentation in the bottle can result in explosions.

NOURISHING
KOMBUCHA RECIPES

II

4
QUICK MIXES

Sometimes you want to dress up your kombucha just a touch without waiting for secondary fermentation to take place. These mixes are quick, simple ways to do just that. Using no more than a few readily available ingredients, these drinks are inexpensive to make and can be thrown together on the fly to create some truly exciting flavor combinations. Perfect for beginners and long-time brewers alike, these mixes can take your original brew up a notch. Mix up a large batch, refrigerate it to have on hand when company stops by, and impress your friends and family with your home-brewed concoction.

GINGER KOMBUCHA

SERVES 2

Put some zip in your step with this combination that brings out the flavor of any type of kombucha. With countless therapeutic properties, including, most notably, its ability to soothe stomachs and inhibit and reduce inflammation, ginger is used as both an herbal medicine and a formidable food flavoring. While this drink tastes great on its own, it can also be added to mocktails, smoothies, and juices in place of plain kombucha for a pungent, spicy twist.

1½ cups kombucha, any type
1-inch ginger knob, peeled

1. Pour the kombucha into a glass.

2. Using a microplane, grate the ginger to create a fine mince.

3. Place the gratings in cheesecloth and squeeze the juice from the gratings into the glass.

4. Stir, pour half of the mixture into a second glass, and serve.

A CLOSER LOOK

It's important to select fresh ginger over ground whenever possible, as it contains higher levels of gingerol, the active anti-inflammatory compound found in ginger. Always inspect fresh ginger before purchasing to ensure it is free of mold and is firm. Store unused, unpeeled ginger in the refrigerator for up to three weeks. For extended storage, place ginger in a freezer-safe bag and store in the freezer for up to six months.

VANILLA KOMBUCHA

SERVES 4

If you enjoy the smooth yet subtle taste of vanilla, this is the drink to try. While it is delicious on its own, especially on a hot day when served over ice, vanilla kombucha can also be added to various mocktails, smoothies, and juices to increase the flavor profile and complement other herbs and spices. Use real vanilla extract for the best flavor. It's best to use a still-sweet batch of kombucha to really play on the vanilla and make its flavor pop.

3 cups kombucha, any type
1 teaspoon vanilla extract

In a large pitcher, add the vanilla extract to the kombucha, stir until blended, and serve over ice. Store any unused vanilla kombucha in the refrigerator for up to 7 days.

DID YOU KNOW?

Vanilla is a type of orchid and the only fruit-bearing plant in the entire species. Native to Central and South America, vanilla was traditionally used as both food and currency in ancient times. Clippings of the plants were taken to Madagascar and French Polynesia, but they did not produce fruit. It was later discovered that a small bee native to Central America was pollinating the vines there, but not those outside the region. To this day, all plants grown outside of Central and South America are hand-pollinated during their brief blooming period. Because of the intensity of labor required to both grow and cure vanilla, it is a premium spice that commands a premium price tag.

BLUSH ROSE KOMBUCHA

SERVES 4

In late spring when strawberries begin to fill market shelves, reach for a pint to make this bright, floral combination. Strawberries are simple to juice by hand, and you can mix this drink in a matter of minutes. Rosewater adds its distinctive floral flavor, and the strawberries blend with it to create a lovely hue of pink that just shines over ice. Rosewater, rich in flavonoids, antioxidants, tannins, and vitamins A, B_3, C, D, and E, not only boosts the taste of this drink but also adds valuable nutrients to increase its overall nutritional value.

2 cups diced strawberries
3 cups green tea kombucha
2 teaspoons rosewater

1. In a small bowl, use a potato masher to mash the strawberries until they are in small pieces and juicy.

2. Pour the mashed strawberries into a wire mesh strainer set over a quart-size jar. Using the back of a spoon, press on the strawberry solids to extract as much juice as possible. Discard the pulp.

3. Add the green tea kombucha to the strawberry liquid.

4. Add the rosewater to the jar, stir, and serve over ice.

A CLOSER LOOK

Rosewater is a by-product in the production of rose oil for use in perfumes and body products. Throughout Asia and Europe, it is widely used to flavor foods. Created in ancient times, rosewater has a distinct flavor that shows up in many Persian and Middle Eastern foods, most notably in sweets such as baklava, rice pudding, and Turkish delight. Find it at your local Indian, Middle Eastern, or Mediterranean grocery store, or check out the Resources section for online vendors.

PEACH KOMBUCHA LASSI

SERVES 2

A lassi is a yogurt-based drink that uses fresh, seasonal fruits to lend sweetness to the otherwise sour notes of plain yogurt. Use oolong or green tea kombucha, both of which have a milder flavor, to allow the delicate sweetness of the peaches to really shine through. Rosewater tops off this cooling favorite with just enough hint of rose to soothe and calm your mind. Even better, the nutritional benefit of kombucha is kicked up a notch when paired with yogurt's probiotic punch.

4 ounces oolong or green tea kombucha
1 ½ cups diced peaches
6 ounces plain yogurt
Splash of rosewater

In a blender, combine the kombucha, peaches, yogurt, and rosewater and blend until smooth. Serve immediately.

PAIR IT
Lassi is typically served in the United States as a sweetened beverage. It's the perfect complement to the spicy food of India, Pakistan, and Bangladesh, where lassi is a traditional drink. The coolness of the yogurt balances the heat of the food. It's also a savory drink that can be flavored with a whole host of spices and flavorings, including cumin, salt, butter, or turmeric. As much a digestive remedy as an enjoyable beverage, a lassi is typically served at lunchtime during hot weather.

CHIA KOMBUCHA REFRESCA

SERVES 2

Once an important food for the Mayans and Aztecs, chia seeds get their name from the Mayan word for "strength" due to their amazing ability to provide sustainable energy. Add chia seeds to this kombucha and sparkling water blend to create a unique texture and give yourself a shot of energy. This burst of nutrients will keep you going strong all afternoon. Because chia seeds take about 15 to 20 minutes to soak up water and be ready for use, be sure to get them started in advance.

1 ounce chia seeds, divided

1 cup water, divided

1 cup black tea kombucha, divided

2 ounces pure fruit juice (apple, cherry, grape, strawberry, etc.), divided

6 ounces sparkling water, divided

1. Divide the chia seeds between two glasses.

2. Add 4 ounces of water to each glass, then let the chia seeds soak for about 15 minutes, until they absorb all the water.

3. Pour 4 ounces of kombucha and 1 ounce of fruit juice into each glass.

4. Divide the sparkling water between the two glasses and serve.

A CLOSER LOOK

Chia seeds aren't classified as a superfood for nothing. They pack in 11 grams of fiber, 4 grams of protein, and 9 grams of fat per 2-tablespoon serving. They are rich in calcium, manganese, magnesium, and phosphorus and surprisingly have only 137 calories per serving. Due to their high protein and fiber content, chia seeds have become a health food champion to support healthy weight loss and control.

HIBISCUS KOMBUCHA COOLER

SERVES 4

This spectacular blend is for hibiscus tea enthusiasts. Combined with mellow green tea kombucha, the flavor of hibiscus comes through in a bold way that will satisfy you any time of the year. Hibiscus tea, known for its deep red color, creates a bright blush cooler when mixed with hay-colored green tea kombucha. Use young green tea kombucha that still has some residual sugar in it to best balance the taste of hibiscus tea, dubbed "sour tea" in its Iranian land of origin.

4 cups water
4 hibiscus tea bags
3 cups green tea kombucha

1. In a small pot, bring the water to a near boil. Turn off the heat.

2. Add the tea bags to the water and cover the pot. Steep the tea for 6 to 8 minutes.

3. Pour the tea into a large jar and refrigerate until thoroughly cooled.

4. Add the kombucha to the cold hibiscus tea and stir to combine. Serve over ice.

DID YOU KNOW?
Hibiscus has long been used throughout Africa and Asia to help maintain body temperature, support heart health and blood pressure regularity, and maintain healthy skin. Up to 30 percent of the hibiscus plant is made up of acids, such as citric acid, malic acid, tartaric acid, and allo-hydroxycitric acid lactone. The drinking of hibiscus tea has been likened to taking blood-pressure medication because it contains anthocyanins, which are believed to be antihypertensive compounds.

CRISP APPLE-ORANGE KOMBUCHA

SERVES 4

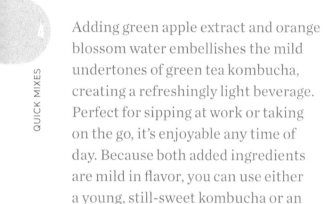

Adding green apple extract and orange blossom water embellishes the mild undertones of green tea kombucha, creating a refreshingly light beverage. Perfect for sipping at work or taking on the go, it's enjoyable any time of day. Because both added ingredients are mild in flavor, you can use either a young, still-sweet kombucha or an older, more soured kombucha to create a drink suited to your personal tastes.

3 cups green tea kombucha
1 teaspoon green apple extract
2 teaspoons orange blossom water

1. In a large pitcher, stir together the kombucha, green apple extract, and orange blossom water until well combined.

2. Serve over ice or refrigerate for up to 7 days.

TRY INSTEAD

If orange blossom water is not available at your local grocery store, look for it at Middle Eastern or Mediterranean grocery stores. If you have trouble sourcing orange blossom water, try 1 teaspoon orange extract and 1 teaspoon water instead. This recipe is also a great opportunity to experiment with other floral waters, such as rosewater.

FROM THE MASTERS

MICHELLE MITCHELL
CO-FOUNDER AND CHIEF CULTURAL ANGEL OF HUMM KOMBUCHA
www.hummkombucha.com

My mother-in-law Barb introduced me to kombucha, as she had been home brewing since the 1980s. Her kombucha, however, tasted horrible—and even she admits it. Drinking Barb's brew was akin to taking a shot of vinegar, and it was necessary to chase it with something, *anything*. But I couldn't argue with the results. For over two decades, she barely caught a sniffle.

In 2002, Barb left for an extended trip, during which time her SCOBY died. Not long after, she caught a particularly nasty virus that never really seemed to go away. For years to follow, she would be laid up in bed for weeks on end—the woman who barely had a sniffle the two decades before. Finally, she got her hands on a SCOBY and began brewing again. In my recollection, she's only been sick once since.

Making the kombucha connection to Barb's health was eye opening. I have no doubt that kombucha holds and transmits a powerful energy, in large part stemming from the joy that those of us who make it "pour" into every bottle. It doesn't require a brewery to make a healing, energy-infused bottle of kombucha. It just takes a combination of natural ingredients and raw enthusiasm. We're all in this together, and the more people who brew and serve their drink to others, the healthier we all are as a community!

5
EFFERVESCENT INFUSIONS

If you like the effervescence of a sparkling beverage, these infusions are for you. Made using the secondary fermentation process, these all require a couple of additional fermentation days to obtain their oh-so-bubbly appeal. The recipes start with simple one-ingredient blends and then delve into more advanced mixtures that play on a variety of flavors. Temperature, amount of sugar, and length of fermentation all affect the development of the carbonation in these drinks.

LEMONADE KOMBUCHA

MAKES 1 GALLON

EFFERVESCENT INFUSIONS

Give the kids down the street a run for their money—or, better yet, an advanced entrepreneurial opportunity—with a lemonade kombucha stand. Lemons kick up the immune-boosting power of probiotic kombucha with flavonoids that help the body fight infection and a boost of vitamin C to cleanse the liver and bowels. This refreshing lemonade kombucha makes for an energizing pick-me-up that tastes as good in the morning as it does at the end of a long day. Cheers!

DID YOU KNOW?

Lemon is a long-standing remedy for fatigue throughout the world. Explorers, world travelers, and long-distance walkers have historically used fresh lemon juice as a quick, refreshing remedy to keep them moving and energized. Quenching thirst more effectively than water, lemon juice also works as an antiseptic and helps protect the body from infection and illness.

1 ¼ cups freshly squeezed lemon juice
15 cups green tea or oolong kombucha

1. Pour 2 tablespoons of lemon juice into each 16-ounce bottle.

2. Using a funnel, fill the bottles with kombucha, leaving about 1 inch of head space in each bottle neck.

3. Cap the bottles tightly.

4. Place the bottles in a warm location, about 72°F, to ferment for 48 hours.

5. Refrigerate 1 bottle for 6 hours, until thoroughly chilled. Open the bottle (over the sink) and taste the kombucha. If it is bubbly to your satisfaction, refrigerate all the bottles to stop fermentation. If it is not there yet, leave the unopened bottles to sit for another day or two and try again. Once your desired effervescence and sweetness are achieved, refrigerate all the bottles to stop fermentation.

6. Strain before serving to remove and discard any yeast strands still present.

ORANGE-FENNEL KOMBUCHA

MAKES 1 GALLON

The orange soda of your childhood memories becomes a grown-up version with a twist—and a whole lot less sugar. A soothing digestive remedy, this soda alternative with orange, ginger, and fennel creates a bubbly masterpiece that will leave you craving more. Blended with black tea kombucha for a robust finish and intense flavor, this show-stopper will likely make its way into your regular rotation.

DID YOU KNOW?

Fennel seeds are widely served on the Indian sub-continent following meals to aid in digestion and eliminate bad breath. Stimulating the secretion of digestive juices and reducing inflammation in the stomach and intestines, fennel is a powerful addition to the diet. Capable of treating anemia, easing indigestion, decreasing flatulence, relieving constipation, preventing heart disease, and promoting brain function, this is one herb you don't want to overlook in your kitchen.

16 cups black tea kombucha
4 tablespoons fennel seeds
3 tablespoons candied ginger, minced
1 tablespoon dried orange peel

1. In a gallon-size jar, add the kombucha, fennel seeds, candied ginger, and dried orange peel.

2. Cover the jar tightly and steep the aromatics at room temperature for 24 hours.

3. Strain the kombucha to remove the herbs.

4. Using a funnel, pour the kombucha into bottles leaving an inch of headspace in the bottle neck. Cap the bottles and place them in a warm location, about 72°F, to ferment for 48 hours.

5. Refrigerate 1 bottle for 6 hours, until thoroughly chilled. Open the bottle (over the sink) and taste your kombucha. If it is bubbly to your satisfaction, refrigerate all the bottles to stop fermentation. If it is not there yet, leave the unopened bottles to sit for another day or two and try again. Once your desired effervescence and sweetness are achieved, refrigerate all the bottles to stop fermentation.

6. Strain before serving to remove yeast strands and flavoring pulp.

CHERRY FAUX SODA

MAKES 1 GALLON

If you are looking for a kid-friendly alternative to soda, this is it. This crowd-pleasing cherry kombucha is a stunning treat on a hot summer evening. Make with a fresh harvest of sweet cherries for a taste of summer. It can also be whipped up using frozen cherries for a midwinter treat when cold weather has you dreaming of warm summer days.

TRY INSTEAD
While black tea kombucha's robust flavor complements the tart-sweet complexity of the cherries, try making this with green or oolong tea kombucha. The milder tones of these teas further intensify the cherry flavor.

14 cups black tea kombucha, divided
32 ounces sweet cherries, pitted

1. In a food processor or blender, purée the cherries along with about 1 cup of kombucha until liquefied.

2. Add the purée and remaining kombucha to a 1-gallon glass jar and cap it with a clean white cloth secured with a rubber band. Leave the jar on the counter in a warm location, around 72°F, for at least 12 hours and no more than 24 hours. The longer it steeps, the stronger the cherry flavor will become.

3. Pour the kombucha through a wire mesh strainer over a large jar or pot to remove any solids.

4. Using a funnel, pour the kombucha into bottles and cap tightly. Place the bottles in a warm location, about 72°F, to ferment for 48 hours.

5. Refrigerate 1 bottle for 6 hours, until thoroughly chilled. Open the bottle (over the sink) and taste the kombucha. If it is bubbly to your satisfaction, refrigerate all the bottles and serve once chilled. If it is not there yet, leave the unopened bottles to sit for another day or two and try again. Once your desired effervescence and sweetness are achieved, refrigerate all the bottles to stop fermentation.

BLACKBERRY ZINGER

MAKES 1 GALLON

Lime juice, a digestive aid in its own right, is used here to add contrast to the blackberries' innate sweetness. Along with increasing the flavor profile from just an everyday fruity beverage to a complex taste explosion, lime juice offers many health benefits, including relief from congestion and nausea, rejuvenation of the skin, reduction of body odor, and the regulation of sugar absorption in diabetic patients. Try this zinger of a drink today, and your body will thank you for it tomorrow.

A CLOSER LOOK

One cup of blackberries contains half of the recommended daily vitamin C that works to protect your immune system. While commercially cultivated in many regions, they also grow wild throughout much of the United States and can be found in the late summer months in fields and along roadsides. Blackberries can be frozen with little effect on their disease-fighting capabilities, making it possible to stock up while these sweet treats are ripe and in season.

2 cups blackberries
4 ounces freshly squeezed lime juice
14 cups black tea kombucha

1. In a large bowl, use a large spoon or potato masher to mash the blackberries and release their juices.

2. Transfer the berries to a gallon-size fermentation vessel and add the lime juice.

3. Fill the remainder of the vessel with the black tea kombucha.

4. Cover the jar using a clean white cloth and secure it with a rubber band. Leave the jar to ferment for 2 days in a warm location, between 68°F and 72°F.

5. After 48 hours, strain the mixture to remove the blackberry seeds.

6. Using a funnel, pour the mixture into bottles and tightly cap them.

7. Leave the bottles in a warm location, about 72°F, to ferment for an additional 2 days.

8. Refrigerate 1 bottle for 6 hours, until thoroughly chilled. Open the bottle (over the sink) and taste the kombucha. If it is bubbly to your satisfaction, refrigerate all the bottles and serve once chilled. If it is not there yet, leave the unopened bottles to sit for another day or two and try again. Once your desired effervescence and sweetness are achieved, refrigerate all the bottles to stop fermentation.

POMEGRANATE KOMBUCHA

MAKES 1 GALLON

Beyond just adding vibrant color, pomegranate offers a pleasant, unique flavor when paired with kombucha. A rich source of antioxidants, including polyphenols, anthocyanins, and tannins, pomegranate is a perfect pairing for this fruity, energizing kombucha. With a tart flavor similar to cranberries, pomegranates have been linked to reducing the risk of chronic diseases, including heart disease and cancer. This recipe uses a combination of black and green teas to create a slightly more delicate, lighter tasting kombucha.

14 cups water, divided
4 black tea bags
4 green tea bags
1 cup sugar
1 SCOBY
2 cups starter tea
1 cup pomegranate juice, divided
2 teaspoons freshly squeezed lemon juice, divided
4 slices fresh ginger, divided

FOR PRIMARY FERMENTATION

1. In a large saucepan, heat 4 cups of water to 212°F over medium heat, then promptly remove the pan from the heat.

2. Add the black and green tea bags, stirring once. Cover the pan and allow the tea to steep for 10 minutes.

3. Remove the tea bags. Add the sugar and stir until all the sugar has dissolved.

4. Pour the remaining 10 cups of water into the saucepan to cool the tea. Check the temperature to ensure that it is below 85°F before proceeding.

5. Pour the tea into a 1-gallon jar.

6. Wash and thoroughly rinse your hands, then lay the SCOBY on the surface of the tea and add the starter tea to the jar.

7. Using a clean white cloth, cover the opening of the jar and secure it in place with a rubber band. Leave the jar in a warm location, around 72°F, to ferment for 7 days.

8. After 7 days, taste the kombucha. If it is too sweet, allow it to ferment for an additional day or two. Once the kombucha tastes good to you, remove and reserve the SCOBY for future use (see page 32). Reserve 2 cups of the kombucha for your next batch before flavoring the rest of the kombucha.

FOR SECONDARY FERMENTATION

1. Line up four 1-quart jars. Add ¼ cup of pomegranate juice, ½ teaspoon of lemon juice, and 1 slice of ginger to each jar.

2. Fill each jar with equal amounts of kombucha, leaving about 1 inch of headspace at the top of each jar.

3. Secure and tighten the lid of each jar and allow the kombucha to ferment in a warm location, about 72°F, for 2 days.

4. Using a funnel, transfer the kombucha to bottles, straining out the ginger as you go. Cap tightly.

5. Chill before serving.

DID YOU KNOW?

While you can make fresh juice when pomegranates are in season, bottled pomegranate juice is available year round. Select unsweetened pomegranate juice when buying bottled juice for this recipe.

EFFERVESCENT INFUSIONS

BLUEBERRY-GINGER KOMBUCHA

MAKES 1 GALLON

Talk about two flavors that were meant to be paired together. Blueberry and ginger are the ultimate health-promoting duo, perfect for any occasion. The sweetness of the blueberry shines through in this bitingly ginger-infused drink that is oh so pleasing. In small amounts ginger is merely a light note of flavor, but it's plentiful here, creating a blend that borders on spicy. Scale up or down the ginger to suit your personal tastes.

TRY INSTEAD

If you don't have candied ginger on hand, substitute a thumb-size piece of fresh ginger. Slice it into matchsticks and place several in each bottle. Alternatively, you can grate it on a microplane, gather the gratings in a piece of cheesecloth, and squeeze the juice among the bottles. Additionally, try a mix of your favorite berries (blueberries, strawberries, blackberries, raspberries, etc.) instead of just using blueberries. This recipe can also be made with a black tea kombucha.

2 cups blueberries
¼ cup candied ginger, chopped
14 cups oolong tea kombucha

1. In a large bowl, use a large spoon or potato masher to mash the blueberries and release their juices.

2. Transfer the berries to a gallon-size fermentation vessel and add the candied ginger and oolong tea kombucha.

3. Using a clean white cloth, cover the jar and secure it with a rubber band. Leave the jar to ferment for 2 days in a warm location, between 68°F and 72°F.

4. After 48 hours, strain the mixture to remove the blueberry and ginger pieces.

5. Using a funnel, pour the kombucha into the bottles and tightly cap them.

6. Place the bottles in a warm location, about 72°F, to ferment for 48 hours.

7. Refrigerate 1 bottle for 6 hours, until thoroughly chilled. Open the bottle (over the sink) and taste the kombucha. If it is bubbly to your satisfaction, refrigerate all the bottles and serve once chilled. If it is not there yet, leave the unopened bottles to sit for another day or two and try again. Once your desired effervescence and sweetness are achieved, refrigerate all the bottles to stop fermentation.

PEACH BLUSH KOMBUCHA

MAKES 1 GALLON

Peaches and summer go hand in hand. While this seasonal blend is best enjoyed at the height of peach season, you can also mix up a batch of this peach, strawberry, and ginger infusion all year long by using frozen or canned fruits. You blend the fruits to create a slurry that you then add to your kombucha for quick and easy infusion. A green tea kombucha really lets the delicate, delectable fruit flavors shine.

DID YOU KNOW?

Peaches aren't used in skin care products just because they smell great. They're actually included in many formulations due to their high level of vitamin C. Vitamin C helps to lessen the appearance of dark circles under the eyes as well as wrinkles. When eaten, peaches are a powerful cleanser for the kidneys, can help with weight control, and are packed with additional vitamins and minerals such as A, E, calcium, iron, magnesium, and zinc.

2 cups diced peaches

4 ounces strawberries

2 ounces freshly squeezed lemon juice

1-inch ginger knob

14 cups green tea kombucha

1. In a food processor or blender, purée the peaches, strawberries, lemon juice, and ginger.

2. Transfer the mixture to a gallon-size fermentation vessel and add the green tea kombucha.

3. Using a clean white cloth, cover the jar and secure it with a rubber band. Leave the jar to ferment for 2 days in a warm location, between 68°F and 72°F.

4. Strain the mixture over a large jar or pot to remove the fruit pieces.

5. Using a funnel, pour the mixture into bottles and tightly cap each bottle.

6. Place the bottles in a warm location, about 72°F, to ferment for 48 hours.

7. Refrigerate 1 bottle for 6 hours, until thoroughly chilled. Open the bottle (over the sink) and taste the kombucha. If it is bubbly to your satisfaction, refrigerate all the bottles and serve once chilled. If it is not there yet, leave the unopened bottles to sit for another day or two and try again. Once your desired effervescence and sweetness are achieved, refrigerate all the bottles to stop fermentation.

MINT KOMBUCHA

MAKES 1 GALLON

Mint brings a delicate, refreshing flavor to kombucha. Bottle the kombucha when it's slightly sweet so that there's still plenty of sugar available during the secondary fermentation process. Enjoy it on its own or use it in mocktails and smoothies to lend a more complex flavor.

DID YOU KNOW?

Mint is typically sold in bunches at the store or farmers' market, and chances are you probably won't use that whole bunch to make kombucha. Store excess mint by cutting off the tips of its stems and placing the mint sprigs in a glass of water like you would cut flowers. Cover the mint with a plastic sandwich bag and place the entire cup in the refrigerator for up to two weeks.

¼ cup fresh mint, coarsely chopped
16 cups black tea kombucha

1. Divide the mint among your 16-ounce bottles.

2. Using a funnel, pour the kombucha into the bottles and tightly cap each one.

3. Leave the bottles on the counter in a warm location, about 72°F, to ferment for 48 hours.

4. Refrigerate 1 bottle for 6 hours, until thoroughly chilled. Open the bottle (over the sink) and taste your kombucha. If it is bubbly to your satisfaction, refrigerate all the bottles and serve once chilled. If it is not there yet, leave the unopened bottles to sit for another day or two and try again. Once your desired effervescence and sweetness are achieved, refrigerate all the bottles to stop fermentation.

CHAMOMILE-LEMON KOMBUCHA

MAKES 1 GALLON

If you like the soothing effects of chamomile tea, you have got to try this! Floral with notes of citrus, this blend is calming and flavorful—just like the tea itself. The lighter tones of green tea kombucha allow the delicate flavor of chamomile to be the star of this drink. Unlike regular chamomile tea, this infusion offers a slight caffeine kick to keep you energized. It's still the perfect remedy for a gray day.

DID YOU KNOW?

Chamomile's anti-inflammatory properties have been used since the times of ancient Greece, Rome, and Egypt. In the Middle Ages it was a common treatment for countless conditions, including asthma, fevers, nausea, and skin diseases. It is also used as a sleep aid and functions as an antipeptic, antispasmodic, antibacterial, antifungal, and antiallergenic agent. When used therapeutically, the flowers are dried and then steeped in a liquid.

4 teaspoons dried chamomile flowers
6 ounces freshly squeezed lemon juice
15¼ cups green tea kombucha

1. Divide the chamomile among the bottles, adding about ½ teaspoon per 16-ounce bottle.

2. Divide the lemon juice among the bottles, adding about 1 tablespoon per 16-ounce bottle.

3. Using a funnel, fill each bottle with the green tea kombucha, leaving about 1 inch of headspace in each bottle neck.

4. Leave the bottles on the counter in a warm location, about 72°F, to ferment for 48 hours.

5. Refrigerate 1 bottle for 6 hours, until thoroughly chilled. Open the bottle (over the sink) and taste your kombucha. If it is bubbly to your satisfaction, refrigerate all the bottles and serve once chilled. If it is not there yet, leave the unopened bottles to sit for another day or two and try again. Once your desired effervescence and sweetness are achieved, refrigerate all the bottles to stop fermentation.

LAVENDER-MINT KOMBUCHA

MAKES 1 GALLON

Mint is a calming, soothing herb that supports healthy digestion. It also serves as a decongestant and sore throat remedy. Its naturally occurring rosmarinic acid has proven effective in relieving seasonal allergies. Lavender supports digestive health as well. It has a floral flavor profile that, when combined with mint, is a great remedy to the heat of summer.

DID YOU KNOW?

While lavender is often thought of as simply a fragrant flower, it is actually an edible herb that has long been used in cooking. Dating back to ancient Egypt, this fragrant herb adds a wonderful floral tone to drinks and other foods. However, keep in mind that a little goes a long way; always err on the side of caution when using this herb. When using dried lavender, use just one-third the amount of fresh lavender called for in a recipe. And always use food-grade lavender, as many florists and nurseries treat lavender with pesticides, rendering them unsuitable for consumption. See the Resources section for where to find lavender.

2 cups water
⅛ cup sugar
½ cup dried lavender buds
⅛ cup chopped fresh mint
14 cups oolong tea kombucha

1. In a small saucepan, bring the water to a boil. Add the sugar, lavender buds, and mint. Stir the mixture for 1 minute, then turn off the heat. Let stand until cool, under 85°F.

2. Strain the mixture and discard the mint and lavender. Add the fragrant water-sugar mixture to a 1-gallon jar, and add the kombucha.

3. Using a funnel, pour the kombucha into bottles. Tightly cap the bottles.

4. Leave the bottles in a warm place, about 72°F, to ferment for 48 hours.

5. Refrigerate 1 bottle for 6 hours, until thoroughly chilled. Open the bottle (over the sink) and taste your kombucha. If it is bubbly to your satisfaction, refrigerate all the bottles and serve once chilled. If it is not there yet, leave the unopened bottles to sit for another day or two and try again. Once your desired effervescence and sweetness are achieved, refrigerate all the bottles to stop fermentation.

FROM THE MASTERS

KIMBERLY LANSKI
OWNER OF BUDDHA'S BREW KOMBUCHA
www.buddhasbrew.com

Meditation is very important to me, so I am hyper aware of what I put into my body and how different foods affect me. A friend of mine introduced me to kombucha, describing it as a living fermented tea. I was immediately intrigued. My first sip of kombucha came from a home brew. I felt my body and senses awaken in a very calm yet energizing way.

I started purchasing kombucha on a regular basis and, as time went on, I decided to brew and bottle my own. It wasn't enough to drink kombucha myself; I wanted to share this amazing beverage with others. The response to my first brews was unbelievable. As requests grew, I found myself brewing nonstop, on a mission to help as many people as possible.

Not long after I began to sell kombucha at farmers' markets, my company, Buddha's Brew Kombucha, was born. Over the years, it has been so gratifying to hear others' stories of how kombucha has helped their bodies. And my own knowledge of and appreciation for kombucha has grown, too. I find it especially fascinating that authentically brewed kombucha contains five to six exclusive probiotic strains that you cannot find in any other food or beverage.

I am forever grateful that I was introduced to kombucha and that it is now such a large part of my life. May your own ongoing home brew practice bring you the balance of energy and calm that I've so cherished since my first taste.

WATERMELON-JALAPEÑO KOMBUCHA

MAKES 1 GALLON

Sweet meets heat in this summer pleaser. The sweetness of the watermelon cuts through the heat of the fresh jalapeño peppers. If you like it hot, add even more jalapeños than the recipe calls for to take this refreshing warm-weather drink to even spicier heights. Regardless of the heat level, this kombucha will pack a punch at your next barbecue.

2 jalapeño peppers, stemmed and halved lengthwise
4 cups diced watermelon
14 cups green tea kombucha

1. Remove the jalapeño seeds, unless you prefer more heat.

2. In a blender or food processor, purée the watermelon.

3. Place a fine mesh strainer over a gallon-size fermentation vessel. Pour the purée into the strainer until all the free-running juice has drained, using a spoon to push through any excess juice from the purée.

4. Discard the purée and add the jalapeño pieces to the watermelon juice.

5. Add the kombucha to the jar and, using a clean white cloth, secure it with a rubber band.

6. Leave the jar in a warm location, between 68°F and 72°F, to ferment for 2 days.

7. Strain the mixture to remove the jalapeño.

8. Using a funnel, pour the mixture into bottles and tightly cap each one.

9. Leave the bottles in a warm location, about 72°F, to ferment for 48 hours.

10. Refrigerate 1 bottle for 6 hours, until thoroughly chilled. Open the bottle (over the sink) and taste your kombucha. If it is bubbly to your satisfaction, refrigerate all the bottles and serve once chilled. If it is not there yet, leave the unopened bottles to sit for another day or two and try again. Once your desired effervescence and sweetness are achieved, refrigerate all the bottles to stop fermentation.

A CLOSER LOOK

Capsaicin, the active ingredient in jalapeños that gives them their spice, has many benefits beyond adding a heat kick to your favorite foods. Capsaicin is an anti-inflammatory used to treat swelling and pain caused by arthritis. It has also been shown to help treat headaches, prevent ulcers, and lower blood pressure.

TART CITRUS-ROSEMARY KOMBUCHA

MAKES 1 GALLON

The tart-sweet goodness of grapefruit is highlighted in this wonderful winter fruit infusion. The additional touch of sugar accelerates fermentation and ramps up the effervescence. Want your kombucha extra bubbly? Include the pulp of the grapefruit in the secondary fermentation for even more carbonation. Rosemary gives the blend a woody, aromatic appeal that helps cut through grapefruit's inherent bitterness. This kombucha is best enjoyed with company next to a warm fireplace or snuggled with a blanket reading a captivating tale.

4 cups water
4 green tea bags
½ cup pure cane sugar
2 tablespoons minced fresh rosemary
2 grapefruit, halved
12 cups green tea kombucha

1. In a small pot, bring the water to a near boil. Turn off the heat.

2. Add the tea bags and steep, covered, for about 8 minutes.

3. Remove the tea bags, pressing them with the back of a spoon against the side of the pot to extract as much tea as possible.

4. Add the sugar to the tea and stir until the sugar is dissolved, then add the rosemary to the tea.

5. Place a wire mesh strainer over the pot and squeeze each grapefruit half to extract the juice, catching any seeds in the strainer.

6. Remove the pulp from one grapefruit half, finely dice it, and add this to the tea. Allow the mixture to cool to room temperature.

7. In a large pitcher or bowl, mix the green tea and pulp mixture with the kombucha.

8. Using a funnel, pour the mixture into bottles and tightly cap each bottle.

9. Leave the bottles on the counter in a warm location, about 72°F, to ferment for 48 hours.

10. Refrigerate 1 bottle for 6 hours, until thoroughly chilled. Open the bottle (over the sink) and taste your kombucha. If it is bubbly to your satisfaction, refrigerate all the bottles and serve once chilled. If it is not there yet, leave the unopened bottles to sit for another day or two and try again. Once your desired effervescence and sweetness are achieved, refrigerate all the bottles to stop fermentation.

DID YOU KNOW?

Grapefruit are best when in season, from winter through early spring. Look for those that are firm, yet slightly springy when gently squeezed. Avoid thick-skinned and wrinkly grapefruit, instead choosing those that appear heavy for their size, meaning they have a thinner skin and more juicy flesh. Grapefruit are juiciest when stored at room temperature, so leave them out if you plan on eating them within a week. If not, refrigerate them for two to three weeks.

RAZZPEARY-GINGER KOMBUCHA

MAKES 1 GALLON

Summer raspberries and autumn pears combine to give you the taste of both seasons. The pears' subtle yet distinctive flavor shines through the milder tones of green tea kombucha. Low in acid and easy on the digestive system, pears create a smooth texture in a way that few other fruits do. Raspberries bring their intense color and sweetness to round out the drink, while the ginger provides just enough flavor to be assertive yet not overpower. Together all these elements create a soothing, delicious tonic for any time of day.

2 pears, cored
1-inch ginger knob, peeled
1 cup raspberries
14 cups green tea kombucha

1. Slice each pear into 8 wedges.

2. Slice the ginger into enough strips to allow for 1 in each bottle.

3. Add 2 pear wedges, 1 ginger slice, and 3 or 4 raspberries per 16-ounce bottle. Be sure the pear wedges fit easily into the bottles so when it is time to clean the bottles, they will easily come out. If the wedges are too wide, slice them lengthwise.

4. Using a funnel, fill the bottles with the kombucha, leaving 1 inch of headspace in each bottle neck. Tightly cap each bottle.

5. Place the bottles in a warm location, about 72°F, to ferment for 48 hours.

6. Refrigerate 1 bottle for 6 hours, until thoroughly chilled. Open the bottle (over the sink) and taste your kombucha. If it is bubbly to your satisfaction, refrigerate all the bottles and serve once chilled. If it is not there yet, leave the unopened bottles to sit for another day or two and try again. Once your desired effervescence and sweetness are achieved, refrigerate all the bottles to stop fermentation.

7. Strain before serving.

A CLOSER LOOK

Raspberries belong to the Rosaceae family of plants, which includes apples, apricots, blackberries, cherries, peaches, pears, and strawberries. Unlike many members of their family, raspberries are very perishable and should be bought only a day or two in advance of consuming. When buying berries in a prepackaged container, check to make sure they aren't overstuffed, as this can cause mold and mashing. If you don't plan on eating raspberries within a day or two, freeze them in a single layer on a baking tray. Once frozen, pack them into a freezer-safe bag or container and return them to the freezer. Store frozen raspberries for up to one year.

ELDERBERRY-SPICED KOMBUCHA

MAKES 1 GALLON

A member of the huckleberry family, the elderberry has been popular for centuries as both a curative and culinary ingredient. They most often are available commercially in their dried form, meaning they are sweeter than when fresh because their sugars are concentrated. Whether you drink this blend for its immune-boosting power or simply because it tastes great, this blend has a complex yet welcoming flavor.

DID YOU KNOW?

Rosehips are the rounded portion of the rose flower positioned just below its petals. The rosehip holds the seeds of the rose plant. Containing a healthy dose of vitamin C, rosehips also contribute to the immune-boosting power of this blend, as they are well known for their ability to treat and prevent cold and flu (as are elderberries). Additionally, rosehips have been used as a stomach tonic for a variety of digestive disorders and to treat high cholesterol, diabetes, high blood pressure, and gout.

1-inch ginger knob
⅓ cup elderberries
¼ cup rosehips
15 cups black tea kombucha

1. Slice the ginger into thin, even strips so that each bottle has at least 1 piece.

2. Divide the elderberries, rosehips, and ginger strips among the bottles.

3. Using a funnel, fill each bottle with the kombucha, leaving a 1-inch headspace in each bottle neck.

4. Place the bottles in a warm location, about 72°F, to ferment for 48 hours.

5. Refrigerate 1 bottle for 6 hours, until thoroughly chilled. Open the bottle (over the sink) and taste your kombucha. If it is bubbly to your satisfaction, refrigerate all the bottles and serve once chilled. If it is not there yet, leave the unopened bottles to sit for another day or two and try again. Once your desired effervescence and sweetness are achieved, refrigerate all the bottles to stop fermentation.

6. To serve, use a wire mesh strainer to remove the aromatics when pouring the kombucha into a glass.

CHILE-LIME KOMBUCHA

MAKES 1 GALLON

Sweet, tart, and spicy combine in this Mexican-inspired kombucha. While two jalapeño peppers give this drink a bite without creating a spicy mouth feel, if you prefer an intense heat, increase the number of peppers. Bottled lime juice works fine, but fresh offers a more in-your-face taste and fresher flavor. To offset the spice, serve cold or on ice. Then sit back, close your eyes, and you'll think you're south of the border.

TRY INSTEAD

Jalapeños just don't do the trick for you? Kick things up a notch further by adding a habañero or Thai pepper to the mix. The heat from these peppers should knock the socks off you.

2 jalapeño peppers, stemmed and halved lengthwise
1½ cups freshly squeezed lime juice
14½ cups black tea kombucha

1. Divide the lime juice among the bottles, adding 2½ tablespoons per 16-ounce bottle.

2. Remove the seeds from the jalapeño, unless you prefer more heat. Cut the jalapeño halves into smaller slices. Add 1 slice of jalapeño pepper per bottle.

3. Using a funnel, fill the bottles with the kombucha, leaving 1 inch of headspace in each bottle neck.

4. Leave the bottles in a warm location, about 72°F, to ferment for 2 days.

5. Refrigerate 1 bottle for 6 hours, until thoroughly chilled. Open the bottle (over the sink) and taste your kombucha. If it is bubbly to your satisfaction, refrigerate all the bottles and serve once chilled. If it is not there yet, leave the unopened bottles to sit for another day or two and try again. Once your desired effervescence and sweetness are achieved, refrigerate all the bottles to stop fermentation.

6. To serve, pour the kombucha through a strainer to remove the jalapeño peppers. If desired, keep the peppers in the drink as a garnish. Serve cold or over ice.

ROOT BEER KOMBUCHA

MAKES 1 GALLON

There's nothing like a frosty mug of root beer. Here, a blend of sarsaparilla root, wintergreen leaf, vanilla, and lime reimagines one of the most classic, storied nonalcoholic drinks. Make this with a young kombucha that still has plenty of sweetness to best play off the flavors of the blend. Unlike in many other root beer recipes, sarsaparilla root and wintergreen leaf are the only ingredients here that will require sourcing from a specialty vendor. Check out the Resources section for some information on where to find these ingredients to get your homemade root beer up and running.

FOR THE ROOT BEER INFUSION

6 cups water
2 ounces sarsaparilla root
¼ teaspoon wintergreen leaves
4 ounces cane sugar
1 tablespoon molasses
1 teaspoon vanilla extract
2 tablespoons freshly squeezed lime juice

FOR THE KOMBUCHA

3 cups root beer infusion
12 cups black tea kombucha

TO MAKE THE ROOT BEER INFUSION

1. In a medium pot, bring the water, sarsaparilla root, and wintergreen leaves to a boil.

2. Reduce the heat and simmer for about 20 minutes.

3. Using a wire mesh strainer, strain the herbs from the liquid and discard the herbs.

4. While the liquid is still warm, add the sugar, molasses, vanilla extract, and lime juice, stirring until the sugar is dissolved.

5. Store this infusion in the refrigerator in a tightly capped jar for up to two weeks. This makes 6 cups.

1. Using a funnel, add ⅓ cup of the root beer infusion to each 16-ounce bottle.

2. Fill the bottles with the kombucha, leaving 1 inch of headspace in each bottle neck. Tightly cap each bottle.

3. Place the bottles in a warm location, about 72°F, to ferment for 48 hours.

4. Refrigerate 1 bottle for 6 hours, until thoroughly chilled. Open the bottle (over the sink) and taste your kombucha. If it is bubbly to your satisfaction, refrigerate all the bottles and serve once chilled. If it is not there yet, leave the unopened bottles to sit for another day or two and try again. Once your desired effervescence and sweetness are achieved, refrigerate all the bottles to stop fermentation.

A CLOSER LOOK

Infusions using sarsaparilla have a storied history as a favorite drink of cowboys in the American West. However, the plant's root has long been used medicinally to treat wide-ranging conditions, including psoriasis and other skin diseases, rheumatoid arthritis, kidney disease, and digestive disorders. Chemicals present in sarsaparilla are thought to help decrease joint pain, itching, and inflammation, as well as protect the liver against toxins.

SPICED KOMBUCHA

MAKES 1 GALLON

The smell of spiced apple cider evokes memories of autumn in a way that few other smells do. This kombucha infusion builds on that nostalgia with a blend of black tea kombucha, apple juice, cinnamon, and clove. It takes on a strong, invigorating flavor after just a couple days of secondary fermentation. This infusion can be served either at room temperature or cold, and it pairs nicely with a donut or other pastry, just like that apple cider from childhood.

DID YOU KNOW?

The timeless adage that "an apple a day keeps the doctor away" may not be as relevant when talking about apple juice as compared to a whole apple. However, there are still many health benefits to drinking apple juice. While there is no definitive evidence, research suggests that apple juice consumption increases acetylcholine in the brain, which may result in improved memory.

1 cup apple juice

4 cinnamon sticks, broken in half

8 whole cloves

2-inch ginger knob, peeled and sliced into 8 thin strips

14 cups black tea kombucha

1. Divide the apple juice among your bottles, adding about 2 tablespoons per 16-ounce bottle.

2. Add 1 cinnamon piece, 1 clove, and a ginger slice to each bottle.

3. Using a funnel, fill each bottle with the kombucha, leaving 1 inch of headspace in each bottle. Seal tightly.

4. Place the bottles in a warm location, about 72°F, to ferment for 48 hours.

5. Refrigerate 1 bottle for 6 hours, until thoroughly chilled. Open the bottle (over the sink) and taste your kombucha. If it is bubbly to your satisfaction, refrigerate all the bottles and serve once chilled. If it is not there yet, leave the unopened bottles to sit for another day or two and try again. Once your desired effervescence and sweetness are achieved, refrigerate all the bottles to stop fermentation.

6. Strain using a wire mesh strainer before serving.

JUNIPER-CITRUS KOMBUCHA

MAKES 1 GALLON

Juniper berries are notable in their ability to remove excess water from the body and are commonly used to help clear congestion caused by colds. Combined with orange juice and its vitamin C kick, this is a great winter infusion for maintaining your good health. And on top of that—it tastes great! Just a couple berries per bottle adds a lovely woodsy, balsamic flavor. This is surely a blend to get you through the long cold and flu season.

DID YOU KNOW?

Juniper berries come from a shrub that grows up to about six feet in height. They have been used widely in herbal medicines, most notably by the Native American tribes of North America. The Blackfoot tribe used a decoction of the berries to treat lung disease, while the Woodland Cree smoked the berries to control asthma. Combined with other berries, needles, and twigs, the Inuit used juniper to prevent and treat colds and flu.

2 cups freshly squeezed orange juice
1 tablespoon juniper berries
14 cups black tea kombucha

1. Add about 4 tablespoons of orange juice to each 16-ounce bottle.

2. Divide the juniper berries evenly among the bottles.

3. Using a funnel, fill the bottles with kombucha, leaving 1 inch of headspace in each bottle neck. Tightly cap each bottle.

4. Leave the bottles in a warm location, about 72°F, to ferment for 2 days.

5. Refrigerate 1 bottle for 6 hours, until thoroughly chilled. Open the bottle (over the sink) and taste your kombucha. If it is bubbly to your satisfaction, refrigerate all the bottles and serve once chilled. If it is not there yet, leave the unopened bottles to sit for another day or two and try again. Once your desired effervescence and sweetness are achieved, refrigerate all the bottles to stop fermentation.

6. Strain before serving.

HOPPY KOMBUCHA

MAKES 1 GALLON

Beer lovers, this one's for you. While it's not really a beer, it has the hoppy flavor of one without all the alcohol. As with all herbal infusions, a little goes a long way. This is a light infusion for a lightly hoppy kombucha. If you prefer the solid hop experience of an India pale ale, experiment by adding a bit more hops to the infusion. It's important to use a young kombucha that still has plenty of residual sugar in it to achieve the carbonation needed to rival that of beer. And if you're looking for a way to take your hoppy kombucha to the next level, check out the simple recipe on page 112 using this kombucha to create a Kombucha Shandy mocktail.

A CLOSER LOOK

Hops can be very strong and bitter when left to infuse for long periods, which is why this recipe has a quicker infusion time than many of the other recipes. If you find this too bitter for your taste, cut back the infusion time to three or four hours. Look for Cascade, Chinook, or Willamette hops for solid flavor, or use an extract made from hop pellets. Check out the Resources section for some home-brew shops with a wide supply of all the hops you will ever need.

¼ cup dried hops
16 cups green tea kombucha

1. Add the dried hops and the kombucha to a gallon-size fermentation vessel.

2. Using a clean white cloth, cover the vessel and secure it with a rubber band.

3. Leave the kombucha at room temperature for up to 8 hours.

4. Using a wire mesh strainer, strain the kombucha to remove the hops.

5. Using a funnel, fill each bottle with the kombucha, leaving a 1-inch headspace in each bottle neck. Tightly cap each bottle.

6. Place the bottles in a warm location, about 72°F, to ferment for 48 hours.

7. Refrigerate 1 bottle for 6 hours, until thoroughly chilled. Open the bottle (over the sink) and taste your kombucha. If it is bubbly to your satisfaction, refrigerate all the bottles and serve once chilled. If it is not there yet, leave the unopened bottles to sit for another day or two and try again. Once your desired effervescence and sweetness are achieved, refrigerate all the bottles to stop fermentation.

MANGO-CAYENNE KOMBUCHA

MAKES 1 GALLON

This combination is a taste of the Caribbean without ever leaving your kitchen. Enjoy this warm sweetness alongside a meal or on its own. Here, the finished product is more sweet than spicy, but if you prefer something a little hotter, add up to ¼ teaspoon more cayenne to create a kombucha that will warm your entire body.

A CLOSER LOOK

Cayenne and other chile peppers are used in traditional Chinese and Ayurvedic medicines to increase appetite and decrease circulatory problems. Cayenne is available in powdered forms for eating and in creams for use topically. Eating cayenne regularly in food preparations can help you burn extra calories, suppress hunger, and minimize chronic pain.

2 cups diced mango
¼ teaspoon cayenne pepper
14 cups green tea kombucha

1. In a blender or food processor, purée the mango.

2. Add the cayenne pepper to the mango and pulse a few times to blend.

3. Divide the purée among the bottles, adding about 2 tablespoons to each 16-ounce bottle.

4. Fill each of the bottles with the kombucha, leaving about 1 inch of headspace in each bottle neck. Tightly cap each bottle.

5. Leave the bottles in a warm location, about 72°F, to ferment for 2 days.

6. Refrigerate 1 bottle for 6 hours, until thoroughly chilled. Open the bottle (over the sink) and taste your kombucha. If it is bubbly to your satisfaction, refrigerate all the bottles and serve once chilled. If it is not there yet, leave the unopened bottles to sit for another day or two and try again. Once your desired effervescence and sweetness are achieved, refrigerate all the bottles to stop fermentation.

7. To serve, strain the kombucha through a wire mesh strainer to remove the fruit pulp as you pour it into a glass.

TANGERINE KOMBUCHA

MAKES 1 GALLON

Citrus flavors pair perfectly with kombucha, and the options really are endless. The bright taste of tangerine comes through full force in this one-ingredient infusion. Oolong tea is best here, where its light, delicate features peek out from behind the immense tangerine flavor. Great tasting on its own, this drink is also delicious in the Kombucha Kosmo mocktail on page 115. Make tangerine kombucha at the height of the small fruit's season, which tends to peak around Thanksgiving, to create a blend bursting with flavor and immune-boosting vitamins.

1 cup freshly squeezed tangerine juice
14 cups oolong tea kombucha

1. Add about 2 tablespoons of tangerine juice to each 16-ounce bottle.

2. Fill each bottle with kombucha, leaving 1 inch of headspace in each bottle neck. Tightly cap each bottle.

3. Place the bottles in a warm location, about 72°F, to ferment for 48 hours.

4. Refrigerate 1 bottle for 6 hours, until thoroughly chilled. Open the bottle (over the sink) and taste your kombucha. If it is bubbly to your satisfaction, refrigerate all the bottles and serve once chilled. If it is not there yet, leave the unopened bottles to sit for another day or two and try again. Once your desired effervescence and sweetness are achieved, refrigerate all the bottles to stop fermentation.

A CLOSER LOOK

Tangerines are smaller than oranges and have a looser peel, making them an ideal snack for adults and children alike. To add more fruit to your diet, purchase a bag of these and keep them in the refrigerator for a quick and juicy snack at home, work, or on the go.

BLACKBERRY-SAGE KOMBUCHA

MAKES 1 GALLON

Sage has many uses beyond your Thanksgiving stuffing. Sage and blackberries are perfectly savory and sweet when combined in kombucha, especially with the immense effervescence created during secondary fermentation. A refreshing dark red infusion, this is a crowd pleaser and a lovely way to introduce kombucha to the uninitiated.

A CLOSER LOOK

Sage is a medicinal herb with a history dating back to the ancient Egyptians, who used the plant as a fertility drug. Most commonly used to treat sore throat, hoarseness, and gastrointestinal distress, the plant has also been used to alleviate such wide-ranging conditions as mouth ulcers and abscesses, staph infections, and menopause.

2 cups blackberries
2 tablespoons fresh sage, sliced into thin strips
14 cups green tea kombucha

1. In a large bowl, use a potato masher or spoon to mash the blackberries until they release much of their juice.

2. Add the blackberries, sage, and kombucha to a 1-gallon fermentation vessel.

3. Using a clean white cloth, cover the jar and secure it with a rubber band.

4. Leave the entire jar to ferment for 2 days in a warm location, about 72°F.

5. Strain the mixture and discard the blackberry pulp and sage.

6. Using a funnel, pour the mixture into bottles, leaving about 1 inch of headspace in each bottle neck. Tightly cap each bottle.

7. Leave the bottles on the counter in a warm location, about 72°F, to ferment for 48 hours.

8. Refrigerate 1 bottle for 6 hours, until thoroughly chilled. Open the bottle (over the sink) and taste your kombucha. If it is bubbly to your satisfaction, refrigerate all the bottles and serve once chilled. If it is not there yet, leave the unopened bottles to sit for another day or two and try again. Once your desired effervescence and sweetness are achieved, refrigerate all the bottles to stop fermentation.

6
JUICES

Juices are a great way to get a boost of vitamins and minerals into your body quickly and efficiently. When coupled with kombucha, juices are sure to provide plenty of probiotics. Because juices have more natural sugar, these drinks tend to be sweeter than the infusions, where much of the added sugar is used during the fermentation process. Whether you're juicing at home or simply want to add a store-bought blend to your homemade kombucha, these recipes have you covered. Offering a sampling of juice recipes that run the gamut of fruits and vegetables, this chapter includes juice blends that can be made using a juicer as well as several that can be made manually with some basic kitchen tools.

CRAN-APPLE KOMBUCHA JUICE

SERVES 1

Cranberry and apple make for a delicious breakfast accompaniment. This drink can be mixed and ready to go in a matter of minutes. Easily scale up the recipe for a crowd. For home juicing, buy cranberries in the fall when they're in season and freeze them until you're ready to use them. Simply thaw them before adding them to your juicer, and you're ready to go. While sweet apples produce a delicious juice that mixes well with the tart cranberries, if you prefer tart apples, try juicing Granny Smith or another not-so-sweet variety.

4 ounces black tea kombucha

4 ounces apple juice

2 tablespoons unsweetened cranberry juice

In a glass, stir together the kombucha, apple juice, and cranberry juice until well combined, and enjoy.

A CLOSER LOOK

Cranberries are a great source of phytonutrients, including phenolic acids, anthocyanins, and flavonoids. Known for their antioxidant, anti-inflammatory, and anticancer properties, cranberries provide the most value when consumed raw, making juicing them a powerful option. Cranberries can also provide extra benefit to the body in their ability to prevent bacteria from adhering to the urinary tract lining, naturally preventing and treating urinary tract infections.

GINGER-PEAR-PINEAPPLE KOMBUCHA JUICE

SERVES 1

Pineapple kicks the sweetness of this blend up a notch with its plentiful natural sugars, while ginger gives it a spicy, pungent taste that plays so well off the acidity of the kombucha. Green tea kombucha is used here, as it highlights the flavors of the natural juices best with its milder qualities and floral notes.

2 firm pears, cored
¼ pineapple, peeled and chopped
½-inch ginger knob, unpeeled
4 ounces green tea kombucha

1. In a juicer, juice the pears, pineapple, and ginger together, placing the ginger between the two fruits to ensure its complete juicing.

2. Stir the juice together with the kombucha and serve.

DID YOU KNOW?
Pears are one of the easiest-to-digest and most hypoallergenic foods known to humans. Pears are highly perishable when ripe, so select firm pears at the store to allow for a day or two of maturing at home. Avoid squeezing the whole fruit, but instead gently press at the top of the pear to determine ripeness. If a pear has become overripe and is squishy, do not use it for juicing.

CANTALOUPE-BASIL KOMBUCHA FRESCA

SERVES 1

Borrowed from the Spanish language, *agua fresca* literally translates to "fresh water" and typically includes just water, fruit, and sugar. Here, the water is replaced with kombucha, and the cantaloupe's orange, juicy flesh serves as the backdrop for the intense flavors of basil and lemon. Made with the more delicate oolong tea kombucha to give the drink a refined flavor, this is a perfect all-ages choice for a summer barbecue or family gathering on a hot day. Scale the recipe up to create a large pitcher to have on hand at your next get-together; you'll be glad you went the extra mile.

A CLOSER LOOK

Because cantaloupes are often picked when unripe to allow for transport, selecting a ripe one can be challenging. First, pick one up. If it feels heavier than expected, that's a good thing, as it can be a sign of ripeness. Second, tap your fingers on its surface and listen. If the sound is deep and dull, it's most likely ripe. If it's higher pitched, it's not. Finally, check the stem-end of the melon by lightly pressing your thumb on it. If it gives slightly, you have found your melon. If it's soft and squishy, it has passed its peak; if firm, it's not ripe.

1½ cups chopped cantaloupe
1 tablespoon freshly squeezed lemon juice
1 tablespoon fresh basil leaves, torn
4 ounces oolong tea kombucha

1. In a food processor or blender, purée the cantaloupe.

2. Place a wire mesh strainer over a bowl and line it with cheesecloth.

3. Pour the purée into the strainer. Once the free-flowing juice drains out, gather the cheesecloth together and gently squeeze the remaining juice out. Discard the pulp.

4. Add the lemon juice and torn basil to the mixture. Steep the juice at room temperature for 1 to 2 hours. Depending on your personal taste, the basil can be picked out or strained from the mixture at this point or left in.

5. Stir the juice together with the kombucha and serve over ice.

GRAPE KOMBUCHA JUICE

A kid favorite, this is also a great one for anyone who's not a huge fan of plain kombucha on its own. The strong flavor and sweetness of the grape is balanced by the sour tang of kombucha. Purple grapes will provide a healthy dose of flavonoid antioxidants along with your kombucha while green grapes offer a plentiful supply of phytonutrients. If you're watching your sugar intake or simply don't like overly sugary drinks, substitute 1 to 2 ounces of spring or carbonated water for an equal amount of the juice to lighten it up.

4 ounces white or purple grape juice
4 ounces kombucha, any type

In a glass, mix the juice and kombucha together and serve.

A CLOSER LOOK

Worldwide over 30,000 square miles of land are cultivated to grow grapes, producing 150 trillion pounds of grapes a year. Make sure you're getting 100 percent grape juice when buying frozen or prepared juices, as anything not labeled as such isn't going to be real juice. When juicing from fresh grapes, remove the grapes in small clusters as you need them instead of pulling individual grapes off the stem, to prevent the stem from drying out and shortening the shelf life of the remaining grapes.

6

JUICES

AÇAI BERRY BURST
KOMBUCHA JUICE

SERVES 1

Açai fruit comes from the açai palm tree, native to Central and South America. The inch-long reddish-purple fruit boasts a brightly colored juice that rivals the antioxidant punch of blueberries, blackberries, strawberries, and raspberries. Here, the sweet açai juice is combined with another nutritional powerhouse, spirulina, to create a juice blend that not only gives you a healthy dose of vitamins and minerals but also works to keep you fuller longer to promote appetite control. If you can't find açai juice near you, look for an açai-blueberry juice blend, a more common and less expensive blend that creates a lovely complement to kombucha as well.

4 ounces açai berry juice
4 ounces black tea kombucha
½ teaspoon spirulina powder

In a glass, mix the juice, kombucha, and spirulina powder together and serve.

DID YOU KNOW?

Spirulina is a microscopic blue-green algae that grows in freshwater ponds and lakes. An amazing source of nutrients, vitamins, and minerals, the powdered form contains up to 70 percent protein, making it an all-around nutrient-dense food. High in chlorophyll, spirulina detoxifies the blood and helps improve immune function. It also aids mineral absorption, lowers cholesterol, and helps support healthy skin, teeth, bones, and eyes. Its high iron content also makes it a good choice to help control anemia.

JUICES

SALTED-GRAPEFRUIT KOMBUCHA JUICE

SERVES 1

Pink is the sweetest variety of grapefruit, and a adding a pinch of salt enhances its flavor in the same way it does for watermelon or cantaloupe. To extract the most juice from a grapefruit, juice it when it's at room temperature and chill the juice before serving. If you do not have a citrus juicer, simply squeeze the grapefruit halves firmly over a glass, using a wire mesh strainer to catch the seeds and any pulp. Use a young kombucha here that still has a bit of sweetness to enhance the flavor of the juice.

4 ounces pink grapefruit juice
4 ounces black tea kombucha
Pinch sea salt

In a glass, mix the juice, kombucha, and salt together and serve.

A CLOSER LOOK

When possible, use fresh grapefruit to make this juice instead of bottled or frozen juice. While many types of juice are labeled as being 100 percent juice, often additional preservatives have been added. Additionally, pasteurization, while helpful to prevent bacteria, mold, and viruses from infecting the juice, also kills valuable enzymes, minerals, and vitamins, minimizing the effectiveness of drinking the juice in the first place.

JUICES

6

ORANGE KOMBUCHA JUICE

SERVES 1

Combine the perennial morning favorite, orange juice, with your home-brewed kombucha to start your day with a healthy dose of vitamins B and C. Kombucha and orange juice can both have varying levels of acidity, and using a young kombucha with a modest hint of sweetness takes this juice to new heights. Choose mandarin oranges, blood oranges, or tangerines for a really sweet juice.

Juice of 2 large oranges
4 ounces black tea kombucha

In a glass, mix the juice and kombucha together and serve cold.

A CLOSER LOOK

While oranges themselves pose little risk for food-borne illness, unpasteurized orange juice has been linked to *Salmonella* contamination. In these cases, it's thought the bacteria were introduced from the exterior of the orange to its internal flesh through cutting, peeling, or juicing. It's important to rinse oranges under running water and then dry them before peeling or cutting to prevent contamination.

JUICES

MINTED APPLE CIDER KOMBUCHA

This low-sugar twist on apple cider is all the fun, without any of the guilt. Mint brings a complexity to the blend for a little something extra special. Look for a natural apple cider that has not been pasteurized during apple season in the fall for the best taste and nutritional profile.

3 cups black tea kombucha
1 cup apple cider
¼ cup loosely packed mint leaves

1. In a large pitcher, mix the apple cider and kombucha together.

2. Stack the mint leaves on top of one another and slice into thin strips.

3. Add the mint to the apple cider kombucha. Steep in the refrigerator for at least 30 minutes, or as long as 3 days.

4. Serve cold, over ice if desired.

DID YOU KNOW?

Apple cider typically refers to unpasteurized and unfiltered apple juice in the United States. However, this product can also be sold as apple juice, and in other cases filtered and clarified juice is also sold as apple cider, further confusing the situation. To purchase true apple cider, look for a small producer or farm in your area that presses apples on the premises for the best flavor and product.

JUICES

CARROT-BEET CLEANSE KOMBUCHA

SERVES 2

Aloe vera juice is thought to decrease irritation and enhance healing of the digestive tract, making it a great accompaniment to this cleansing kombucha smoothie. The combo of beet, carrot, and apple juice is a liver-cleansing trio that can dramatically improve health when taken regularly. First, the carrots alkalize the body and help flush the liver. The beets come in with their high levels of phytonutrients to provide strong antioxidant and anti-inflammatory quality to stimulate detoxification. And finally, the apple, a general body detoxifier, is rich in pectin, which binds to toxins in the intestines for excretion and lowers the workload on your liver. Add the kombucha, and this is a probiotic cleansing party you don't want to miss.

4 medium carrots
1 medium beet
1 large green apple
4 ounces black tea kombucha
1 ounce aloe vera juice

1. In a juicer, juice the carrots, beet, and apple.

2. In a medium pitcher, mix the juice together with the kombucha.

3. Stir in the aloe vera juice and mix until combined. Serve.

DID YOU KNOW?
While it's best to make fresh juice every time you drink it, in a pinch it can be stored for a short period of time when done properly. Refrigerate fresh juice for up to eight hours in a clean glass jar, such as a canning jar, with a tight-fitting lid. However, keep in mind that once you make fresh juice, it almost immediately begins losing some of its vitamin and nutritional content through oxidation, so don't wait too long to drink it!

TANGERINE-CARROT KOMBUCHA

SERVES 2

The stronger, woody taste of black tea kombucha mixed with the bright orange color of tangerine carrot juice is smooth and delicious for any time of the day. Drink this in winter to boost your immunity or in summer for a refreshing start to a warm day. Whatever you do, make sure you use tangerines to give the drink its characteristic flavor that only they can offer.

6 small tangerines
4 medium carrots
4 ounces black tea kombucha

1. In a juicer, juice the tangerines and carrots.

2. In a medium pitcher, mix together the juice with the kombucha and serve cold.

A CLOSER LOOK

Carrots are an excellent source of beta-carotene and other antioxidants that support cardiovascular and vision health. One of the most popular root vegetables in the United States, carrots are most recognizable in their bright orange color; however, they are also found in a wide variety of colors, including purple, yellow, white, and red. Store carrots in the refrigerator wrapped in a plastic bag to prevent moisture loss during storage for up to two weeks. If you buy carrots with their stems and greens attached, remove these before storage, as they can pull moisture from the carrots and cause them to prematurely deteriorate.

7
BLENDED DRINKS

Kombucha adds an invigorating nutrient booster for your daily smoothie, adding just the perfect tang to really stand out. Blend it with fruits, vegetables, or a combination of the two to create a meal in a glass that not only tastes great but offers additional health benefits for your body as well. Experience a taste explosion with these mouth-watering combinations that can help you fight off a cold, boost your immunity, and give you an extra shot of energy for a long afternoon at work. Whatever your fruit or vegetable preference, a smoothie is a great way to include kombucha in your diet and get a healthy dose of vitamins and minerals all in one glass.

BLUEBERRY-LIME KOMBUCHA SMOOTHIE

SERVES 1

Relive summer all year long with this smoothie that perfectly matches the sweetness of blueberries with the bold and piquant essence of lime. The included banana helps you stay fuller longer, and the black tea kombucha's earthy flavor provides a strong complement of acidity. Using frozen fruits eliminates the need to add ice to create the classic smoothie texture.

1 cup frozen blueberries
4 ounces black tea kombucha
½ frozen banana
Juice of 1 lime

In a blender, purée the blueberries, kombucha, banana, and lime juice until smooth, about 10 seconds. Pour into a glass and serve.

DID YOU KNOW?

Blueberries are at their peak season in the United States from May through October. Find a farm near you to pick blueberries during these months and freeze them for use throughout the winter. Freezing doesn't damage any of the blueberry's anthocyanin antioxidants, and u-pick farms offer considerable price breaks when you come and pick fruit yourself, making this a win-win situation. An extra bonus—you get a healthy dose of vitamin D in the process.

MANGO-LEMON KOMBUCHA SMOOTHIE

SERVES 1

Whether a cold winter day or a hot summer one, this drink will surely take you on a tasty journey to the islands. Find frozen mango at the grocery store, or cube and freeze it yourself. The earthy tones of black tea kombucha add a delectable complexity to the smoothie, and its higher caffeine level makes it a great choice when you need a little added energy.

1 cup frozen mango
4 ounces black tea kombucha
½ frozen banana
Juice of 1 lemon

In a blender, purée the mango, kombucha, banana, and lemon juice until smooth, about 10 seconds. Pour into a glass and serve.

PAIR IT
This smoothie pairs perfectly with Caribbean cuisines. It's the perfect accompaniment for the bold flavors of a Jamaican jerk chicken or subtler preparations of fish and seafood.

7

BLENDED DRINKS

FRUITY KALE
KOMBUCHA SMOOTHIE

SERVES 1

High in iron and vitamin K, a kale smoothie is a great way to start the day. Get a blast of powerful antioxidants from both the kale and fruit to boost your immune function and cardiovascular health. The coconut oil in this meal in a glass provides a healthy dose of fat to help keep you full longer.

4 ounces kombucha, any type

1 cup kale, stems removed

1 banana, fresh or frozen

½ cup frozen fruit (blueberries, strawberries, peaches, mangoes, etc.)

1 tablespoon extra-virgin or virgin coconut oil

Pinch cinnamon

In a blender, blend the kombucha, kale, banana, frozen fruit, coconut oil, and cinnamon for about 45 seconds on high, until smooth. Pour into a glass and serve.

TRY INSTEAD

To pile on the goodness, further fortify the nutritional punch, and kick up this meal in a glass, consider adding one or more of the following to this smoothie: 1 cup spinach; 1 teaspoon minced ginger; 1 tablespoon chia seeds; 1 tablespoon spirulina, hemp, or other superfood; and 1 teaspoon honey or maple syrup. Find the combination or combinations that satisfy your tastes.

STRAWBERRY-BANANA KOMBUCHA SMOOTHIE

SERVES 1

Strawberry-banana is a classic pairing, elevated here with the inclusion of the sweet and sour kombucha. Banana gives the smoothie its characteristic silkiness, while strawberries provide the mouthwatering sweet flavor. Use freshly picked local strawberries when in season to really take this smoothie to new heights.

6 ounces black tea kombucha
1 frozen banana
6 ounces frozen strawberries

In a blender, purée the kombucha, banana, and strawberries until smooth, about 10 seconds. Pour into a glass and serve.

DID YOU KNOW?
Bananas have some amazing health benefits that should not be overlooked. While they are effective in beating muscle cramps in the legs and feet, they can also help with depression. Bananas' high levels of tryptophan, which is converted to serotonin by the body, can help increase levels of this happy-mood neurotransmitter.

GREEN DREAM KOMBUCHA SMOOTHIE

SERVES 1

This green dream smoothie pulls out all the stops to create an amazing drink bursting with sweet indulgence and a healthy dose of vitamins. Spinach is the star ingredient, while avocado lends both a smooth creaminess and its light green hue. Mango and apple give the smoothie plenty of subtle sweetness. Scale this up and make enough for everyone, as inevitably, once they taste it, they will most certainly want their own.

1 handful spinach
½ apple
½ avocado
4 ounces black tea kombucha
2 tablespoons frozen mango chunks
4 ounces ice

In a blender, purée the spinach, apple, avocado, kombucha, mango, and ice until smooth, about 10 seconds. Pour into a glass and serve.

DID YOU KNOW?
While there are over 1,000 different types of mangoes grown throughout the world, very few are sold commercially in the United States. The Tommy Atkins variety is the most widely sold type and has the characteristic red and green skin. Keep an eye out for Ataulfo mangoes, which are much smaller and have a vibrant yellow color and a small seed, giving them a higher flesh-to-seed ratio than other varieties. These mangoes are typically available in stores from March to July.

STRAWBERRY-PAPAYA KOMBUCHA SMOOTHIE

SERVES 1

Referred to as the "fruit of the angels" by Christopher Columbus, papaya is renowned for its soft, butter-like consistency. Papaya becomes available in stores starting in early summer, falling perfectly in line with strawberry harvests and making them a great pair to combine in a smoothie. Papaya flesh is a rich orange color, creating a hyperbright drink that tastes as good as it looks. Because papaya is not overly sweet, a touch of honey or agave nectar helps bring out its fresh fruit flavor.

4 ounces black tea kombucha
4 ounces frozen strawberries
1 cup diced papaya
1 teaspoon honey or agave nectar

In a blender, purée the kombucha, strawberries, papaya, and honey until smooth, about 10 seconds. Pour into a glass and serve.

DID YOU KNOW?

Papayas, native to Central America, have been cultivated in Hawaii since the 1920s. When purchasing papayas, look for those with reddish-orange skin that's slightly soft to the touch if you plan on eating them within a day. If you want to wait a couple of days, choose those with patches of yellow, signifying that they need more time to completely ripen. Store papayas at room temperature to ripen, or in the refrigerator once fully ripened if they're not to be consumed for a day or two. Like squash, papayas have large seeds that need to be removed before eating. Cut the papaya in half and scoop out the seeds using a sturdy spoon.

BLENDED DRINKS

PINEAPPLE-MINT KOMBUCHA SMOOTHIE

SERVES 1

This smoothie will exceed the recommended daily value of manganese and vitamin C. Why? The healthy dose of pineapple that's included. An apple adds some bulk, and the mint lends a bright freshness to this tropical blend. Black tea kombucha offers the best contrast to the sweetness of the pineapple with its woody flavor, and using a longer fermented kombucha with little residual sugar won't overpower the pineapple's sweetness.

4 ounces black tea kombucha
1 apple, cored and chopped
2 cups frozen pineapple pieces
3 mint leaves

1. In a blender, process the kombucha and apple until liquefied, 10 to 15 seconds.

2. Add the pineapple and mint to the blender and process until smooth, about 10 seconds.

3. Pour into a glass and serve.

DID YOU KNOW?

If you feel a boost in your energy level after eating pineapple, it's for good reason. The trace mineral manganese present in pineapple is an essential cofactor for a number of enzymes that help support energy production and antioxidant defense. Additionally, it's a solid source of the B vitamin thiamin, which is part of the enzymatic reactions that allow the body to produce energy.

COCONUT-STRAWBERRY KOMBUCHA SMOOTHIE

SERVES 1

If coconut is your go-to flavoring for pastries, waffles, and drinks, then this is the drink to try. Creamy bananas, juicy strawberries, and spicy ginger create a rich, satisfying smoothie on their own, but adding coconut to the mix hits it out of the park. Beyond providing a tropical element, the shredded coconut increases the fiber, iron, and fat content of this smoothie, keeping you full longer and promoting healthy digestion. Unsweetened coconut is the best option, limiting your intake of processed sugars.

4 ounces black tea kombucha
½ banana
1 cup strawberries
4 ounces ice cubes
½-inch ginger knob
3 tablespoons shredded unsweetened coconut

In a blender, purée the kombucha, banana, strawberries, ice, ginger, and coconut until smooth, about 10 seconds. Pour into a glass and serve.

DID YOU KNOW?
Once opened, a bag of shredded coconut can deteriorate quickly and even go rancid under the wrong conditions. Store coconut in a tightly sealed bag or other airtight container in the refrigerator for up to six months.

7

BLENDED DRINKS

8
HEALTHY MOCKTAILS

When you want the fancy of a cocktail but the health benefits of kombucha, skip the alcohol altogether and whip up a batch of one of these mocktails. All made virgin, these drinks play on the best elements of a wide range of your favorite drinks but save you the added calories and stress on the body by eliminating the alcohol. As with all cocktails, these are best served in fancy glasses to make a statement without saying a word. While some require steeping or secondary fermentation to get their flavors just right, others can be mixed straightaway to turn any occasion festive in a hurry.

KOMBUCHA MARGARITA

SERVES 2

Whether you prefer it on the rocks or blended, this virgin kombucha margarita has all the zing and none of the added sugar of a typical premade margarita mix. Salt the rims of serving glasses to give mocktail hour an authentic presentation.

PAIR IT

While margaritas are traditionally served with Mexican food, don't be afraid to pair them with other cuisine, as their sweetness and acidity can play well against many other foods. The acid of the lime pairs well with seafood such as shrimp and oysters, while chicken dishes that include fruit-based glazes also work with the sweet beverage. Try serving margaritas with a salad using a lemon or lime vinaigrette or along with barbecued skewers of meats for a twist on the usual food pairings.

2 tablespoons coarse salt
1 lime, sliced
1 ½ cups Ginger Kombucha (page 42)
2 ounces freshly squeezed lime juice
2 ounces coconut water
1 teaspoon agave nectar
Ice (see methods below)

TO PREPARE YOUR GLASSES

1. Pour the salt onto a small plate.

2. Using 1 lime slice, slide it around the rim of the glass to moisten it. Invert the glass and place its rim in the salt, turning slightly. Flip the glass over and set aside.

3. Repeat with the remaining glass. Proceed to make the drink.

ON THE ROCKS

1. Using a cocktail shaker, mix the kombucha, lime juice, coconut water, and agave nectar together.

2. Add ice to your prepared glasses, and pour the drink into each. Garnish each glass with a lime slice and serve.

BLENDED

In a blender, blend the kombucha, lime juice, coconut water, and agave nectar along with 10 to 15 ice cubes until the margarita approaches a slushy consistency. Pour it into the prepared glasses. Garnish each glass with a lime slice and serve.

PIÑA KOMLADA

SERVES 2

Kombucha lends an intricate flavor to the silky piña colada. Use black tea kombucha to create the most complexity in this drink. The pineapple's and coconut milk's sweetness stand up to the kombucha's acidity, and you'll think you're drinking the real thing. This kid-friendly concoction is perfect for a summer party or to transform your winter blues into tropical island fantasies. Serve with a mini-umbrella, and you are well on your way to relaxation street.

2 cups frozen pineapple chunks
6 ounces black tea kombucha
1 cup coconut milk

In a blender, blend the pineapple, kombucha, and coconut milk until smooth, about 10 seconds. Pour into a tall glass and serve.

DID YOU KNOW?

First developed in Puerto Rico in the 1950s, the piña colada had gained prominence in the world of bartending by the following decade. The precursor to the piña colada was made from rum, coconut cream, and coconut milk and was served in hollowed out coconut shells. But after the coconut cutters' union went on strike in San Juan, a bartender at the Caribe Hilton decided to use a hollowed-out pineapple to house the drink, and the piña colada was born.

HEALTHY MOCKTAILS

'BUCH BLOODY MARY

SERVES 4

Sunday brunch and Bloody Marys are practically synonymous. For the 'Buch Bloody Mary, the drink goes through secondary fermentation, packing a probiotic punch into the tomato base and creating a masterful mocktail. Garnish this drink the same way you would a traditional Bloody Mary, with celery, asparagus, pickled beans, or whatever else you prefer.

A CLOSER LOOK

Tomatoes are a rich source of antioxidants, most notably lycopene, which is responsible for the pigmentation of the fruit. Linked to improving heart and bone health, a diet rich in fresh tomatoes helps lower total cholesterol. Also rich in vitamin C and beta-carotene, tomatoes add an immune-boosting punch when combined with kombucha.

2 medium tomatoes, halved
¼ diced cucumber
1 teaspoon chili powder
4 cups black tea kombucha

1. In a blender, purée the tomato and cucumber for about 5 seconds.

2. Stir the chili powder into the mixture.

3. Using a funnel, pour the purée into a large jar or bottle.

4. Add the kombucha to the bottle, leaving a 1-inch headspace. Tightly seal the jar.

5. Leave the jar in a warm location, about 72°F, for 48 hours.

6. Refrigerate for at least 6 hours, then serve chilled with your preferred garnish.

KOMBUCHA FIZZ

SERVES 2

The fizz first made a name for itself as a cocktail in the 1887 edition of *Bartenders Guide*. By the mid-1950s it had become so popular that teams of bartenders would be employed with the sole purpose of shaking the drinks. While traditionally made with gin, the minimalistic cocktail is made throughout the world using scotch, fruit-infused liquors, and rum. This kombucha and lime version creates the acidic base that defines the drink. Mint pairs wonderfully with the flavors to give it an additional note of complexity.

Juice of 2 limes
5 fresh mint leaves, divided
4 ounces black tea kombucha, divided
1 cup sparkling water, divided

1. In a glass, muddle the lime juice and 3 mint leaves. Divide the mixture between two highball glasses.

2. Add 2 ounces of kombucha to each glass.

3. Add ½ cup of sparkling water to each glass, on top of the kombucha.

4. Garnish each glass with a mint leaf and serve immediately.

A CLOSER LOOK

As with other citrus fruits, high doses of vitamin C are a major plus for the lime. The most notable effects of lime include protecting the eyes from macular degeneration, improving digestion, improving weight loss, and relieving constipation. Next time you reach for a lime, be sure to squeeze a few extra wedges onto your food for your health!

RASPBERRY-MINT KOMBUCHA MOJITO

SERVES 2

Mojito, a Cuban drink traditionally made using rum, translates to "something a little wet," and this completely fits the bill. The mojito gets a remake here, replacing the cane sugar with maple syrup, which lends a distinct flavoring that pairs well with the raspberry.

PAIR IT

Enjoy this mocktail with grilled or stewed meats and vegetables for a refreshing and fruity complement to the heavier proteins. Served alone, it also makes for a vibrant nightcap.

2 teaspoons maple syrup, divided

Juice of 1 lime, divided

1 teaspoon grated ginger, divided

Small handful fresh mint leaves, plus extra for garnish

½ cup fresh raspberries, plus extra for garnish

1 cup ice

1 cup black tea kombucha

2 lime wedges, for garnish

1. In each glass, muddle 1 teaspoon of maple syrup, half the lime juice, ½ teaspoon ginger, and half the mint.

2. In a small bowl, mash the raspberries to extract their juice.

3. Place the raspberries in a wire mesh strainer and, using the back of a spoon to press as much juice from the raspberries as possible, divide their juice between the two glasses.

4. Add ½ cup of ice to each glass and fill each with ½ cup of the kombucha.

5. Garnish each glass with a lime wedge, mint leaves, and a few raspberries and serve.

CINNAMON-CHERRY KOMBUCHA MOCKTAIL

SERVES 2

This mocktail is as perfect for the holiday season as a warm summer night. Drawing on the flavors of the cooler seasons—cinnamon and clove—serve it in a martini glass to up its festive side. Because it requires at least 24 hours of steeping to achieve its best flavor, make it a day or two ahead of time.

A CLOSER LOOK

While the research is still inconclusive, some studies have shown that cinnamon can help lower cholesterol and treat yeast infections. Even more studies have shown the spice's ability to reduce inflammation and fight bacteria. For the most benefit, choose Ceylon cinnamon, as opposed to the more widely available cassia cinnamon. While the cost is greater, so are its associated benefits and flavor.

3 cinnamon sticks, divided
4 whole cloves
1 cup Cherry Faux Soda (page 54)

1. In a medium jar or bottle, add 1 cinnamon stick and all the cloves to the Cherry Faux Soda.

2. Place the sealed bottle in the refrigerator and allow the mixture to steep for 24 to 48 hours.

3. Strain the kombucha into two martini glasses, garnish each with a cinnamon stick, and serve.

FRUITY LEMON KOMBUCHA MOCKTAIL

SERVES 2

Sometimes a fruity cocktail is just the ticket after a long day. This is your answer right here. Using any of your favorite fruit-flavored kombucha blends, it is made with lemons to increase the acidity and add a welcome tang, while honey balances the flavors. Berry-based fruit infusions work best here, but feel free to experiment with any of your favorite blends to personalize this drink to your own brews.

A CLOSER LOOK

While lemons can be stored at room temperature, if you don't plan on using them within one week, the refrigerator is your best option. When left out, a lemon loses moisture through its peel, rendering it dried and hardened. Instead, seal lemons in a plastic zippered bag and store in your refrigerator for up to one month.

Juice of 2 lemons
2 tablespoons raw honey
Ice, for glasses
1 cup kombucha, any fruit-infused variety
Fresh fruit, for garnish

1. Divide the lemon juice between two glasses.

2. Add 1 tablespoon of honey to each glass and stir to combine well with the lemon juice.

3. Add ice to each glass.

4. Add ½ cup of the kombucha to each glass.

5. Garnish each drink with fresh fruit as desired and serve.

FAUX GIN AND TONIC

SERVES 4

Infuse juniper berries and lemon peel into the kombucha overnight for this take on the classic gin and tonic. It's a perfect remedy for those hot summer days. Whether you're hanging out in the backyard or lounging poolside, this mocktail will tickle your taste buds.

TRY INSTEAD

Just as there's no one way to make gin, there's also no one way to make gin-flavored kombucha. Consider adding one or more of the following to your juniper berry and lemon peel infusion: a pinch fennel seeds, a pinch allspice, ¼ teaspoon coriander seeds, 1 green cardamom pod, 2 black peppercorns, 1 fresh or dried bay leaf, 1 small rosemary sprig, or 1 fresh lavender sprig. Find the infusions you like best.

1 tablespoon dried juniper berries
1 strip fresh lemon peel
2 cups black tea kombucha
Ice, for glasses
Juice of 2 limes, divided
2 cups tonic water, divided
Lime wedges, for garnish

1. In a large pitcher, add the juniper berries and lemon peel to the kombucha and steep overnight in the refrigerator.

2. Using a wire mesh strainer, strain the kombucha and discard the berries and lemon peel.

3. Fill the glasses with ice and add 4 ounces of the faux gin kombucha and a quarter of the lime juice to each glass.

4. Top each glass with ½ cup of tonic water, garnish each with a lime wedge, and serve.

KOMBUCHA SHANDY

SERVES 4

Beer drinkers unite for this shandy recipe that will actually detox your body. Using ginger simple syrup and hop-infused kombucha, this shandy tastes like the real thing—minus the hangover. Brew a gallon of hop-infused kombucha to have on hand for making this faux shandy whenever inspiration strikes.

DID YOU KNOW?

Once you make a simple syrup, you can store it for future use to make countless drinks and preparations. Cool the syrup to room temperature, pour it into a clean container with a tight-fitting lid, and store it in the refrigerator for several weeks.

FOR THE GINGER SIMPLE SYRUP

1 cup sugar
1 cup water
¼ pound ginger

FOR THE SHANDY

4 ounces ginger simple syrup, divided
4 ounces freshly squeezed lime juice, divided
3 cups Hoppy Kombucha (page 76), divided
4 cups club soda, divided

TO PREPARE THE GINGER SIMPLE SYRUP

1. In a small saucepan, simmer the sugar and water until the sugar is completely dissolved.

2. While the sugar and water are simmering, peel the ginger and cut it into matchstick-size pieces.

3. In a blender, purée the ginger and syrup.

4. Strain the mixture through a wire mesh strainer, using the back of a spoon to press on the ginger solids to extract as much liquid as possible.

5. This makes about 1¾ cups syrup.

TO MAKE THE SHANDY

1. Add 2 tablespoons of ginger syrup and 1 ounce of lime juice to each glass.

2. Add about ¾ cup of kombucha to each glass.

3. Top each glass with 1 cup of club soda and serve.

KOMBUCHA & SODA

SERVES 2

Fans of scotch and soda or vodka and soda will appreciate this version. Simple to throw together in a flash, it's a great one for your chest of mocktails for when company comes calling. Using just five ingredients—kombucha, sparkling water, ice, lemon, and lime—this is one of the easiest mocktails in the book and also one of the best. Gather the ingredients, get to chopping some lemon and lime wedges, and you're almost done.

A CLOSER LOOK

Sparkling water is made simply by carbonating water and has the same hydrating effect as plain water, and many people find it more palatable than flat water. Check the label to watch out for sparkling waters that add sodium and sugars during the flavoring process.

Ice, for glasses
4 ounces black tea kombucha, divided
4 or 6 lemon wedges
4 or 6 lime wedges
8 ounces lemon-lime-flavored sparkling water, divided

1. Add ice to two glasses and pour 2 ounces of kombucha into each glass.

2. Squeeze the juice from 1 or 2 of the lime and lemon wedges into each glass and place the rinds on the glass rims.

3. Top each glass with 4 ounces of sparkling water.

4. Garnish each glass with additional lemon and lime wedges and serve.

OOLONGTINI

SERVES 2

Shaken or stirred? A list of mocktails is not complete without a faux martini. Serve oolongtinis on the rocks or shake the ingredients with ice and serve them chilled straight up. And what's a martini without a garnish? Skewer a couple of olives or cocktail onions to make this drink memorable.

TRY INSTEAD

Oolong kombucha is not the only tea in town for making a faux-tini. Experiment with black tea or green tea kombucha, as both pair great with ginger to produce a full-bodied mocktail with a little more bite. Add a splash of cranberry juice to either drink to make a festive, fruity faux-tini.

6 ounces oolong tea kombucha, divided
2 ounces Ginger Simple Syrup (page 112), divided
Ice, for glasses
Juice of 1 lemon, divided

TO PREPARE ON THE ROCKS

1. In each of 2 glasses, add 3 ounces of kombucha and 1 ounce of ginger syrup to ice.

2. Divide the lemon juice between the two glasses.

3. Stir and serve.

TO PREPARE STRAIGHT UP

1. In a cocktail shaker, combine the kombucha, ginger syrup, ice, and lemon juice.

2. Close the top and mix the ingredients by shaking.

3. Pour the Oolongtini into two martini glasses and serve.

HEALTHY MOCKTAILS

KOMBUCHA KOSMO

SERVES 2

The cosmopolitan is the height of sophistication, and so is this mocktail. Tangerine kombucha replaces the vodka for the perfect holiday tangy drink. Use a cocktail shaker to blend the ingredients and give the drink its authentic chilled appeal. Garnish with a twist of lime zest to add both aesthetics and flavor to this classic cocktail with a virgin twist.

4 ounces cranberry juice
2 ounces freshly squeezed lime juice
Ice, for mixing
4 ounces Tangerine Kombucha (page 78)
2 slices of lime zest

1. In a cocktail shaker, add the cranberry juice, lime juice, and ice to the kombucha and secure the lid.

2. Shake vigorously to mix the ingredients.

3. Pour the kosmo into two chilled martini glasses, garnish each drink with lime zest, and serve.

PAIR IT
Kosmos go great with shrimp, making them a perfect accompaniment to your shrimp dinner. Tempura shrimp or steamed shrimp served with cocktail sauce complement the sweet and sour flavor of the kosmo, as do strongly flavored cheeses such as Brie, aged cheddar, or goat cheese.

THE DIRTY DOZEN & CLEAN FIFTEEN

A nonprofit and environmental watchdog organization called Environmental Working Group (EWG) looks at data supplied by the US Department of Agriculture (USDA) and the Food and Drug Administration (FDA) about pesticide residues and compiles a list each year of the best and worst pesticide loads found in commercial crops. You can refer to the Dirty Dozen list to know which fruits and vegetables you should always buy organic. The Clean Fifteen list lets you know which produce is considered safe enough when grown conventionally to allow you to skip the organics. This does not mean that the Clean Fifteen produce is pesticide-free, though, so wash these fruits and vegetables thoroughly.

These lists change every year, so make sure you look up the most recent before you fill your shopping cart. You'll find the most recent lists as well as a guide to pesticides in produce at EWG.org/FoodNews.

2015 DIRTY DOZEN

Apples	Peaches
Celery	Potatoes
Cherry tomatoes	Snap peas
Cucumbers	Spinach
Grapes	Strawberries
Nectarines	Sweet bell peppers

In addition to the Dirty Dozen, the EWG added two foods contaminated with highly toxic organo-phosphate insecticides:

Hot peppers	Kale/Collard greens

2015 CLEAN FIFTEEN

Asparagus	Mangoes
Avocados	Onions
Cabbage	Papayas
Cantaloupe	Pineapples
Cauliflower	Sweet corn
Eggplant	Sweet peas (frozen)
Grapefruit	Sweet potatoes
Kiwis	

MEASUREMENT CONVERSIONS

VOLUME EQUIVALENTS (LIQUID)

US STANDARD	US STANDARD (OUNCES)	METRIC (APPROXIMATE)
2 tablespoons	1 fl. oz.	30 mL
¼ cup	2 fl. oz.	60 mL
½ cup	4 fl. oz.	120 mL
1 cup	8 fl. oz.	240 mL
1½ cups	12 fl. oz.	355 mL
2 cups or 1 pint	16 fl. oz.	475 mL
4 cups or 1 quart	32 fl. oz.	1 L
1 gallon	128 fl. oz.	4 L

OVEN TEMPERATURES

FAHRENHEIT (F)	CELSIUS (C) (APPROXIMATE)
250°	120°
300°	150°
325°	165°
350°	180°
375°	190°
400°	200°
425°	220°
450°	230°

VOLUME EQUIVALENTS (DRY)

US STANDARD	METRIC (APPROXIMATE)
⅛ teaspoon	0.5 mL
¼ teaspoon	1 mL
½ teaspoon	2 mL
¾ teaspoon	4 mL
1 teaspoon	5 mL
1 tablespoon	15 mL
¼ cup	59 mL
⅓ cup	79 mL
½ cup	118 mL
⅔ cup	156 mL
¾ cup	177 mL
1 cup	235 mL
2 cups or 1 pint	475 mL
3 cups	700 mL
4 cups or 1 quart	1 L

WEIGHT EQUIVALENTS

US STANDARD	METRIC (APPROXIMATE)
½ ounce	15 g
1 ounce	30 g
2 ounces	60 g
4 ounces	115 g
8 ounces	225 g
12 ounces	340 g
16 ounces or 1 pound	455 g

RESOURCES

BOOKS

Childs, Eric, and Jessica Childs. *Kombucha!* New York: Penguin Group, 2013.

Lee, Stephen. *Kombucha Revolution.* Berkeley, CA: Ten Speed Press, 2014.

BLOGS

Cultures for Health blog
blog.culturesforhealth.com/

Donna Schwenk's Cultured Food Life blog
www.culturedfoodlife.com/blog/

The Mountain Rose Blog on Kombucha Brewing
mountainroseblog.com/
brew-kombucha-part-1/

BREWING SUPPLIES AND EQUIPMENT

Cultures for Health
www.culturesforhealth.com
For equipment and starter SCOBY

F. H. Steinbart Company
www.fhsteinbart.com
For a complete kombucha brewing kit

The Kombucha Shop
www.thekombuchashop.com
For a complete kombucha brewing kit
or individual supplies

Mountain Rose Herbs
www.mountainroseherbs.com
For teas, herbs, and spices to use in
your brewing

Savory Spice Shop
www.savoryspiceshop.com.
For herbs, spices, and florals to use in
your brewing

KOMBUCHA COMMUNITIES

Fermenters Club
www.fermentersclub.com

Kombucha Brooklyn
www.kombuchabrooklyn.com/blog/community

Kombucha KommUnity
kombucha.ning.com

REFERENCES

Bauer-Petrovska, Biljana, and Lidija Petrushevska-Tozi. "Mineral and Water Soluble Vitamin Content in the Kombucha Drink." *International Journal of Food Science and Technology* 35 (2000): 201–205.

Cultures for Health. "What's in My Kombucha?" Accessed August 5, 2014. www.culturesforhealth.com/kombucha-yeast-bacteria.

Jaret, Peter. "What Are Probiotics?" Benefits, Supplements, Foods and More." Digestive Diorders Health Center, WebMD. Accessed August 6, 2014. www.webmd.com/digestive-disorders/features/what-are-probiotics.

Mayo Clinic. "Vitamins and Minerals: What You Should Know about Essential Nutrients." *Mayo Clinic Women's HealthSource.* July 2009. Accessed August 6, 2014. www.mayoclinic.org/documents/mc5129-0709-sp-rpt-pdf/doc-20079085.

Stone, Thomas L. "Kombucha Tea." *Nutrition Digest of the American Nutrition Association* 22, no. 1 (Winter 1997). Accessed August 5, 2014. americannutritionassociation.org/newsletter/kombucha-tea.

University of Maryland Medical Center. "Vitamin B_1 (Thiamine)." Accessed August 6, 2014. umm.edu/health/medical/altmed/supplement/vitamin-b1-thiamine.

INGREDIENTS INDEX

INDEX

ABOUT THE AUTHOR

Katherine Green is a writer and food educator
in Portland, OR. She is a fermentation geek,
trained winemaker, and the former owner of
Mama Green's Jam. She lives with her husband,
two sons, and a flock of chickens.

ALSO IN THE DIY SERIES

Making delicious probiotic foods in your own kitchen has never been easier.

AVAILABLE NOW
$12.99 paperback
$6.99 ebook

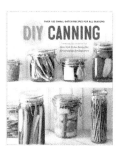

Preserve nature's bounty and enjoy seasonal ingredients throughout the year.

AVAILABLE APRIL 2015
$12.99 paperback
$6.99 ebook

CPSIA information can be obtained at www.ICGtesting.com
Printed in the USA
BVOW07s2119101115

426387BV00005B/7/P